"This book is much needed within the early years' sector
tial positive impact when supporting young children's soc
health (SEMH). As a relatively new term in inclusion, Sonia ...., ...
concepts in an accessible and sensitive manner and links pedagogy with practice.
This book opens up opportunities for practitioners to take proactive and positive steps
to support children in managing their social and emotional experiences and encourages us to also "take a moment" to reflect and decide upon the best approaches for
increasing overall well-being within our early years environments.

One of the most significant aspects of Sonia's book is that she expertly outlines the interaction between adult and child and how our own wellbeing must be
nurtured before we are in the powerful position of nurturing others. She addresses
crucial but challenging topics such as adverse childhood experiences and recognises the importance of a holistic approach to shifting the culture and practice of
well-being and well-doing. She navigates us through these topics with compassion and care, and the book provides a hopeful and achievable way to develop
our skills and knowledge.

This book feels like a much-needed toolkit for anyone working with young children, and through Sonia's extensive knowledge, signposting and interviews with other
professionals, there are plenty of tangible ideas to be put straight into action."

– Kerry Payne, Early Childhood SEND Specialist

"Sonia's expertise as a nurture worker translates itself onto every page and welcomes you into a safe and trusted place to explore a much needed topic on children's social emotional and mental health in the early years.

This book leads with empathy and is woven into the practical ideas and information designed to support early years practitioners support our very youngest
children who need the most amount of care, patience and understanding.

This book is exactly what we have come to expect from Sonia who is leading
and guiding the sector when it comes to emotional wellbeing - it is a must read
and one that should be on the book shelf of every early years setting!"

– Kate Moxley, Early Years Consultant

"In this unique and outstanding book, Sonia Mainstone-Cotton provides an
empathic insight into some very difficult areas of children's physical and mental
health. Her thoughtful and reflective narrative, straight from the heart, ensures
that the children's wellbeing is always paramount. The practical chapters provide
constructive help for all types of settings and circumstances, making it an easy to
use reference book for everyone. A much-needed and beautifully written book."

– Kathy Brodie, author and Early Years consultant

Supporting Children with Social, Emotional and Mental Health Needs in the Early Years

This accessible book offers essential guidance and practical ideas for Early Years staff to support children with social, emotional and mental health (SEMH) needs. It draws upon a wealth of experiences and insights to explore what SEMH is, why children may have SEMH needs, and what this can look like, giving practitioners the confidence they need to understand early signals and signs.

Chapters share practical tools, activities and strategies, exploring topics that include:

▶ environment
▶ routines and transitions
▶ sensory experiences
▶ feelings and emotions
▶ the role of the adult.

A range of case studies and resource suggestions are woven throughout, bringing the theory alive with first-hand advice from a variety of professionals, including educational psychologists, play therapists and Forest School specialists. This book is a refreshing and practical guide, and an essential read for all Early Years practitioners looking to cultivate a supportive and compassionate environment.

Sonia Mainstone-Cotton is a freelance nurture consultant. She currently works in a specialist team supporting 3- and 4-year-olds who have social, emotional and mental health needs. Sonia also trains staff across the country, working with children's centres, schools, nursery, charities and churches.

Supporting Children with Social, Emotional and Mental Health Needs in the Early Years

Practical Solutions and Strategies for Every Setting

Sonia Mainstone-Cotton

Routledge
Taylor & Francis Group

LONDON AND NEW YORK

First edition published 2021
by Routledge
2 Park Square, Milton Park, Abingdon, Oxon, OX14 4RN

and by Routledge
605 Third Avenue, New York, NY 10158

Routledge is an imprint of the Taylor & Francis Group, an informa business

British Library Cataloguing-in-Publication Data
A catalogue record for this book is available from the British Library

Library of Congress Cataloging-in-Publication Data
Names: Mainstone-Cotton, Sonia, author.
Title: Supporting children with social, emotional and mental health needs in the early years: practical solutions and strategies for every setting / Sonia Mainstone-Cotton.
Description: First edition | Abingdon, Oxon; New York, NY: Routledge, 2021. | Includes bibliographical references and index. | Summary: "This accessible book offers essential guidance and practical ideas for early years staff to support children with social, emotional and mental health (SEMH) needs. It draws upon a wealth of experiences and insights to explore what SEMH is, why children may have SEMH needs, and what this can look like, giving practitioners the confidence they need to understand early signals and signs. Chapters share practical tools, activities, and strategies, exploring topics that include: Environment Routines and transitions Sensory experiences Feelings and emotions The role of the adult A range of case studies and resource suggestions are woven throughout, bringing the theory alive with first-hand advice from a variety of professionals, including educational psychologists, play therapists and forest school specialists. This book is a refreshing and practical guide, and an essential read for all early years practitioners looking to cultivate a supportive and compassionate environment"– Provided by publisher.
Identifiers: LCCN 2020057192 (print) | LCCN 2020057193 (ebook) | ISBN 9780367545147 (hardback) | ISBN 9780367545123 (paperback) | ISBN 9781003089544 (ebook)
Subjects: LCSH: Children with mental disabilities–Education (Early childhood) | Children with social disabilities–Education (Early childhood) | Emotions in children. | Social skills in children.
Classification: LCC LC4602.5 .M35 2021 (print) | LCC LC4602.5 (ebook) | DDC 371.92–dc23
LC record available at https://lccn.loc.gov/2020057192
LC ebook record available at https://lccn.loc.gov/2020057193

ISBN: 978-0-367-54514-7 (hbk)
ISBN: 978-0-367-54512-3 (pbk)
ISBN: 978-1-003-08954-4 (ebk)

Typeset in Optima
by Deanta Global Publishing Services, Chennai, India

Thank you, Iain, for your ongoing support and all your encouragement in my work with children and in my writing.

Thank you to the NOS team – you are the best team to work with.

Contents

Acknowledgements

Thank you to

- ► Judith Parr
- ► Nicky Spencer-Hutchings
- ► Ruth Fergusson
- ► Fred Lacey-Ford
- ► Kieran McCarthy
- ► Sharon Cooke
- ► Andy Hattersley
- ► Ed Harker

for your interviews, wisdom and insight.

Introduction

This book focuses on how we support young children's social, emotional and mental health (SEMH), especially those children who have higher needs in this area. I work for a specialist team in Bath called Threeways Brighter Futures and am part of their Nurture Outreach Service team (NOS). This is a service that supports Reception-aged children in their transition from pre-school to school, throughout their Reception year and across the transition into Year 1. The children we work with have all been identified as needing additional support with their social, emotional and mental health; they have all been recognised as having high needs in this area. We work with the child once a week all year; our work is about supporting the child but also offering ideas, suggestions and support to the education staff who are with the child each day. Our work is only made possible by having staff in schools who trust us and are willing to try out and implement our ideas. Throughout this book, I have included interviews from members of the NOS team, so I may share with you their knowledge, wisdom and experience.

The term 'social, emotional and mental health' (SEMH) is relatively new. We increasingly hear it in schools, but there is a growing recognition of this term within the Early Years. I think it is important for us to view SEMH within a model of difference rather than one of deficit. We are all on a SEMH needs continuum, and we all need to have our SEMH needs met. As educators, we need to support children's SEMH needs wherever we find them.

Early Years practitioners are often the first to see and wonder if a child may need additional support with their SEMH needs. However, there is very little information specifically for them on this subject. There are a growing number of books looking at general wellbeing for children, and I have written some of these. However, I was aware of the need for one that looks at specific ways to support children who have additional SEMH needs. My hope for writing this book is to start providing some information that may supply Early Years practitioners with ideas to support, plan and work with children and their SEMH needs. This book is not about diagnosing a child, but it *is* about shining a light on what is happening for a child, and an encouragement to be curious and ask questions about what the child might be experiencing and how they are showing us their needs. Children will tell us when they have SEMH needs, but they often do not use words to let us know. Our job is to understand that they are communicating to us in many different ways and we need to try to understand what they are telling us and then find ways to support them.

Social, emotional and mental health needs are recognised as one of the four areas under the umbrella of SEND (special education needs and disability). Sometimes there are overlaps between these areas, with some children displaying a mix of needs. If SEND is a new area for you and you are interested in how SEMH fits into this, I would encourage you to do some further reading and research. Kerry Payne is a great person to look at and learn from in the area of SEND (see the link in 'Further information and references' for a webinar with her).

This book has two sections. The first includes Chapters 1 to 4, which offer thoughts around the subject of SEMH and children's experiences. These chapters are quite heavy at times, as they explore difficult subjects, such as adverse childhood experiences (ACEs), attachment, abuse, trauma, parental mental health difficulties, drug and alcohol misuse, domestic violence and the role of the adult. Due to the heavy nature of these chapters, you might want to take breaks while reading this and take care of yourself and decide to move into Section II (Chapters 5 to 12), which comprises more practical topics. Each of these look at ways we can support children with SEMH needs, offering ideas and many practical suggestions and resources that may help you in your work. This second section looks at a mix of areas, from the environment, recognising feelings and emotions, and sensory play, to being outside, mindfulness, working with parents and how we can support our wellbeing. The book can be read all the way through, or you may want to dip in and out of different chapters for practical tips and ideas.

My hope is that the book will offer you some ideas and suggestions and will give you some background information about how we can work with children who may have additional SEMH needs. I have added boxes at the end of each chapter, giving suggestions for further reading or learning. My intention is this book will enable you to see that we can all make a difference to children's SEMH needs, and that there are small but important tweaks and changes we can all make that will help these children to thrive.

I am aware that I work in a specialist team and the ideas I am sharing in the book are based on my experience and some reflections from the team. When we work with the children, we do not have a one-size-fits-all model; our work is based on trying to meet the individual needs of each child and to support their education staff to feel empowered and enabled to do this. The ideas I share are not about a model that can be replicated across the country, but hopefully they will give you some ideas and encouragement to try out some of the suggestions and find your own creative ways of supporting children with SEMH needs.

I started to write this book in April 2020, when the country, and much of the world, was in lockdown due to the Covid-19 pandemic. Currently, I am acutely aware of the stress and anxiety this is causing for many families. We know that when we all return to normality there will continue to be ongoing scars across the United Kingdom and the world as an outcome of this period. I'm fairly certain we will see an increase in the number of children who are going to have social, emotional and mental health needs, and I hope this book will offer you some information about SEMH, along with practical ideas about how to support children with SEMH needs.

 Further information and references

Kerry Payne – Supporting children with SEND. Available at https://kinderly .co.uk/early-years-webinars/

Social, emotional and mental health needs in children

Part I: Exploring trauma, ACEs and the impact of stress on the body

This chapter explores the category of social, emotional and mental health (SEMH). It is a relatively new category that is increasingly being used across disciplines – for example, health, education and social care. It is a phrase we often hear about school-aged children, however, there is a growing recognition that Early Years children are also displaying some higher social, emotional and mental health needs. I will also explore adverse childhood experiences (ACEs), and briefly look at attachment theory too, as these both play a crucial part in helping us to understand and think about SEMH.

A quick definition of children with social, emotional and mental health needs could be:

- children who find it extremely difficult to manage their feelings, emotions and behaviours
- children who find everyday change challenging and frightening
- children who find it difficult to build relationships with adults and or children
- children who find it hard to join in the activities and routine with the rest of the class/group.

Some of the behaviours you might see in children who have more SEMH needs are:

- violent outbursts to adults and or other children
- distress because the parent or key person is not with them
- running off
- refusal to join in or follow instructions

- needing to be in control and controlling things around them
- frozen behaviours, where they appear to shut down
- hiding
- withdrawing from adults and or children
- self-harming
- being easily startled by loud noises, sudden movement, doors slamming
- anxiety
- prolonged temper tantrums
- sleeping difficulties.

A recent NHS survey (2018) showed that one in eight children aged 5 to 19 in England had a mental health disorder. It also looked at pre-school children aged 2 to 4 years (the first time this younger age group has been surveyed) and found that one in eighteen children aged 2 to 4 years had at least one mental health disorder. The survey was carried out with 9,117 children and young people, parents and teachers, and its aim was to hear about children and young people's mental health from a range of voices: the children and young people themselves and also adults who know them. They divided mental health disorders into four categories:

- emotional
- behavioural
- hyperactivity
- less common disorders.

Note: I wouldn't usually use the term 'disorder'. However, it was used in this survey, as they did not screen for general mental 'health problems' or 'issues' (NHS Digital 2018).

TAKE A MOMENT

Before we go any further, I would like to encourage you to take a moment to think about the earlier list of behaviours. As you take another look at the list, consider whether it reminds you of any particular children you either currently work with or have worked with?

Going on the figures of the NHS Digital survey, it is very likely we are all currently working with children who are experiencing a mental health difficulty, as 1 in 18 for children aged 2 to 4 years is a high number. This book is not suggesting that we diagnose these children – that is not our role – but we must be aware of the possibility that some of the children we work with may have additional SEMH needs. Once we are aware of this, we can begin to ask questions, make links with relevant agencies, and there are some things we can put in place that will help all children, especially those who may be experiencing additional SEMH needs.

TAKE A MOMENT

Your wellbeing

This is a difficult subject to read about. It may bring up strong feelings in you about children you currently work with or have worked with, or it may bring up feelings and emotions about your children or your childhood. Your wellbeing is crucial. While you are reading this book, I would like to encourage you to be mindful about the feelings it is raising in you. Be kind to yourself. If you are finding this difficult or triggering, take some time to nurture yourself. This might be by making yourself a cup of tea, giving yourself a hand massage, doing a five-minute meditation, or speaking to a friend or trusted colleague. Looking after your own wellbeing is crucial, as it enables you to support children's wellbeing. This is a subject I will explore more in Chapter 12.

Some descriptions used for children with SEMH needs highlight that they may have experienced toxic stress or they may have experienced trauma. We now recognise that a one-off traumatic incident, such as a car accident, will not cause the same effect as long-term traumatic events or toxic stress. Toxic stress impacts our biology: it leads to a disruption in our stress responses, resulting in what is often seen as dysregulated behaviours and distrust of others (Bombèr 2020). However, it is worth noting that not all children who have experienced trauma or toxic stress go on to develop higher social, emotional and mental health needs. Some children are very resilient and we know that, where children have a positive, loving, safe connection with an adult, this can contribute to their resilience. It is also important to be aware that not every child who displays SEMH needs will have experienced trauma or toxic experiences.

I am now going to look at some of the known reasons why some children might experience higher SEMH needs and may have encounter toxic stress.

ACEs

'ACEs' (adverse childhood experiences) is a term that many will now be familiar with. The initial thinking around ACEs began in 1985 in an obesity clinic in San Diego. Dr Vincent Felitti (Felitti et al. 1998), who led the Department of Preventive Medicine, was questioning why so many of his adult patients were dropping out of the weight loss plan. He began to interview patients and discovered a pattern of what he would later describe as adverse childhood experiences. He started to hear stories from patients about the abuse they experienced in childhood. Felitti and his colleagues went on to interview another 100 patients, finding this to be a common story. From this initial research, he and his colleagues proceeded to lead the original ACE study. Epidemiologist Robert Anda teamed up with Felitti, and together they devised the questions for the ACE study. This questionnaire had 10 questions based around adverse childhood experiences, and these are still used to measure an ACE score. They asked patients if, before the age of 18, they had lived through any of the experiences listed. The questions look at 10 areas:

- emotional abuse
- physical abuse
- verbal abuse
- sexual abuse
- neglect
- substance abuse in the house
- mental illness in the household
- domestic violence
- divorce or parental separation
- criminal behaviour in the household.

Each category counted as one point (Burke Harris 2018). A list of the full questionnaire can be found on the Center on the Developing Child, Harvard University website (2015; see 'Further information and references'). Since its initial development, the questionnaire is now being looked at worldwide. There is also now an International ACE Research Network. This forms part of the World Health Organization, which has developed an ACE-IQ (2018), the aim of which is to facilitate the measurement of childhood adversities in all countries and compare adversities between them, enabling them to discover the links between childhood adversities, health risk behaviours and health outcomes later in life. The suggestion for the International ACE-IQ is to use it alongside broader health surveys. This survey has a lot more detail in it, breaks down each of the initial questions and asks more detailed questions. For example, there is a section on specific types of physical punishment: 'Did a parent, guardian or other household member spank, slap, kick, punch or beat you up?' 'Did a parent, guardian or other household member hit or cut you with an object, such as a stick (or cane), bottle, club, knife, whip etc.?' It also breaks down the answers into categories – 'Many times', 'A few times', 'Once', 'Never', 'Refused'. The survey also has a section on peer violence, community violence and exposure to war. You can find details about this and a copy of the survey on the World Health Organization website (see 'Further information and references').

In the initial Felitti and Anda study, 17,421 people were asked the ACE questions. They found that ACEs were common and that one in six of all the respondents had an ACE score of four or higher. They realised that adverse experiences are often interrelated: although they are often researched separately, Felitti and Anda found that in practice they rarely stand alone. When they looked at these results more closely, they began to see that the effects of childhood trauma started to be evident when children were in school. They discovered that over half of those with ACE scores with four or higher disclosed how they had learning or behavioural difficulties in school. This was compared to three per cent of people who scored a zero. They also discovered that those people with a higher ACE score had a greater risk to their health. As the ACE score rises, the rates of chronic depression in adulthood rose and they also found those with a score of four and above had a far greater chance of suffering from heart disease, cancer, liver disease and chronic lung diseases. They concluded that stress on the body continues having a long-term impact (Burke Harris 2018, van Der Kolk 2014).

Our understanding of the study

The study led to a greater and deeper understanding of the impact adverse childhood experiences can have on our lives in the longer term. One of the leading figures informing the world and helping people not only to understand ACEs, but also how we can help to alleviate their impact, is Dr Nadine Burke Harris, a paediatrician in San Francisco. She did a TED Talk in 2014 and also went on to write *The Deepest Well: Healing the Long-Term Effects of Childhood Adversity* (2018). In the book, she examines the impact these early traumas have, both during childhood and later into adulthood, but she also looks at how her clinic is helping to heal those traumas, exploring how we can stop the initial traumas and what can help to stop the long-term consequences. Burke Harris used the ACE questions with the parents of her child patients at her outpatient clinic. She found that, with her child patients (average age 8), those who had four or more ACEs were twice as likely to be overweight and 32.6 times more likely to have a diagnosis of learning and behaviour difficulties. This contributed to giving Burke Harris the evidence to show that many of the children she was seeing who'd been told they had a 'behaviour problem' had difficulties directly linked with experiences of toxic adversity. She argued this finding was crucial in being able to give the children the correct diagnosis and support. She found large numbers of children in her clinic were being diagnosed with ADHD. However, Burke Harris felt that a lot of these children were showing signs of a chronic negative impact on their stress response systems, which is different to straight ADHD (Burke Harris 2018).

Questions around ACEs

Since the study, many people wordwide have been interested in and aware of ACEs, and discussion in both health and education sectors has increased. In the United Kingdom, Scotland has taken the lead in understanding this, but also highlighting concerns with using just ACEs and recognising the pitfalls with this approach. An increasing number of people are raising caution about using ACEs alone or, as Barrett (2018) describes it, the growing 'ACE-aware movement'. She and others emphasise that the initial ACE study was part of a health survey – it was never intended for clinical, education, Early Years or charity workers to use its questions as a tick-box questionnaire with parents or children. Barrett is an education psychologist and, along with others in her profession, suggests that the tick-box exercise is a potentially harmful practice. They point out that there is more to trauma than the event itself. The way it impacts children and adults is different for everybody and is dependent on so many different factors, such as where they live, the support they have, previous experience and their health. There is also a concern that we should be extremely cautious when using these questions with families, as it may act to re-traumatise them (Barrett 2018).

How an understanding of ACEs helps us

It is important to have an understanding of the lives of the children we are working with and what their everyday experience is. For example, when we know that a child has lived with domestic violence, we then have a greater understanding if the child is very jumpy, hypervigilant and can become very violent. With this information, we can offer the child the safety, love and support they need. However, I agree with Whitney Barrett and others who raise caution at the judgements that can be made by using ACEs and of the danger of categorising children. Public Health Scotland (2021) does not recommend that anyone uses the questionnaires with adults or children to 'gather' ACE scores, as there is a concern that this can lead to unhelpful stigmatisation and could upset or unsettle families.

It is important to remember that there can be many things in a child's life that contribute towards them experiencing additional SEMH needs. The categories on the ACE list give some indication, but they don't always give us a full picture. For example, living in violent areas, moving suddenly lots of times, being homeless, living in chronic poverty, having a parent or a sibling with a chronic long-term illness, being bullied or your family experiencing bullying can all cause extreme stress to a child and their family, yet these don't make the list.

In our team, we try to understand the story of the child and family we are working with, but we do this by building a relationship with them, by meeting them, coming alongside them and letting them know that we are there to work with them and support them, not to judge them. I find the idea of asking families a list of very personal questions on a first meeting incredibly invasive, and it has the potential for us to come over as very judgemental. When we first take on a new child, some information will be shared from other professionals – for example, if there is known domestic violence or if there is a history of drug use with the parents. On a first meeting with parents, one of my openers is always 'Can you tell me something about your child that brings you joy.' Often – not always, but often – parents delight in telling me something positive about their child, as they are usually expecting to have to tell professionals the negative things. I will ask parents if there are things I need to know about life at home, say, but this is done through a conversation. I recognise that there is a skill in that. I have worked with parents for over 25 years, I have learned how to sit and be, how to hopefully not be judgemental or shocked by things I hear and to be able to give the space for parents to feel they can talk about what life is like. But I don't push for information, as I recognise that will come over time. It can sometimes be after almost a

13

year of working with a parent that they feel they can say they have experienced violence, mental health issues or bullying from their neighbour.

With the children we work with, we are aware that the initial information we hear is only part of their story, but it can help shine a small light on some of the things the children are experiencing and showing us through their behaviour. In our experience, some of the children we work with don't appear to have experienced any ACEs or other traumas, and yet they may still be showing regular signs of distress and dysregulation, anxiety or fear.

To help us understand how ACEs can help inform Early Years practitioners, I am going to include an excerpt of an interview with Judith Parr. Judith is a children's centre coordinator and works for the local authority where our team is based, in Bath and North East Somerset.

Why do you think it's helpful for Early Years practitioners to have an understanding of ACEs and trauma?

It is vital if we know what we are working with, if we know the situations that children in our care are facing daily; then we can come up with tools or use the tools that are out there, to help them build resilience to manage what they are dealing with. We mostly cannot change things when we are talking about ACEs. We can do our best to protect children from harm and abuse but, when we are talking about parental incarceration and parental mental health issues, also wider issues that we don't see named on the ACEs list, e.g. community deprivation, poverty, etc. We can't change those, but we can work with families to help them build resilience for their children, and make sure those children have the resources they need to get through it. We know for every child it takes a village to raise a child and if we can be part of that village, in whatever format that takes for those very young children, we can also be the village for their families. We know if we can support adults who are facing adversity, that will have a beneficial effect to the children.

Can you explain how this information can enable Early Years practitioners to make a difference?

Research from the original study in ACEs in America and further studies has shown that there are things that make a difference to children. Having an adult outside the family who believes in you, being present to someone, being visible. For children to go into a nursery or a school and be noticed, this makes a huge difference to a child. Within the Early Years, we know that having the foundation of social, emotional development in the Early Years is massively influential on a child through the rest of their life. If we teach resilience in the Early Years, it will help them as they develop through life. We know that when children are resilient, they are better able to cope with whatever life throws at them. We can teach children resilience, how to manage problems, and how to help children to manage a tolerable level of stress, giving them the tools to help them. We need to be proactive, Early Years practitioners who see children every day or several times a week, are key in being the positive adult outside the home, who can foster a love of learning and play and can help children cope with problem-solving.

How to support families when we know life is challenging

Judith describes how we can be part of the village that raises the child and I like this image. I think it is so important to remember that we can offer support, a listening ear to families. As Early Years providers, we may also be the first place that families go to be signposted for further help. We always need to be clear about what we can and cannot do, and knowing the agencies in your area who can offer support and guidance is important. Over the years I have heard of some excellent examples of Early Years settings that are supporting parents to think about how they can parent. I know some nurseries who have a lending library of useful parenting books, such as those by Dan Siegel and Tina Payne-Bryson (2020) and Margot Sunderland (2016). Books help parents to reflect on their parenting style in light of the way they were parented. I know other nurseries that have made links with local children's centres and signpost families to parenting courses. They also make information available to parents on their website or in their newsletter, such as local support groups for mental health difficulties, domestic violence, and so on.

Stress on the body

What is clear about traumatic experiences is that it can cause toxic stress. I mentioned toxic stress and how this can harm the body earlier on in this chapter. To help us understand the impact stress can have on the body, I interviewed Nicky Spencer-Hutchings. Nicky is a member of our Brighter Futures team. She works with adoptive children and families and also delivers Thrive (2021) training across the country.

Could you explain how ongoing stress from experiences such as ACEs impacts the brain and the body?

Children's survival is solely dependent on an adult meeting their basic needs. For many adults, for many real reasons, they can find it very hard to meet their children's needs. Often it is the child who needs to adapt to the situation in most extraordinary ways to stay alive and keep their caregiver in just enough contact with them so they survive. This certainly is surviving but not thriving,

When a child experiences ongoing, chronic and frequent exposure to traumatic experiences that impact on their or their caregiver's sense of safety, it can have an immediate and long-term impact on their growing bodies and brains. This is called toxic stress. This is very different from the everyday challenges that a child needs in normal healthy development to promote resilience and growth.

Could you explain a bit more about toxic stress?

Toxic stress occurs in situations of neglect, abuse, exposure to domestic violence, and many examples of serious experiences that can occur within the family. When children's sense of safety is compromised, their bodies prepare to protect themselves and respond to danger by releasing chemicals that trigger a fight/flight or freeze response. This evolutional response to danger is designed for an adult to respond to the immediate danger of, for example, a wild animal in their path. It isn't designed for a small child scared by the violence they are witnessing in their home. This fight/flight and freeze and neurobiological response is rushing through their systems but, because of their size, it doesn't equip them to stop the threat. Instead, they unconsciously learn sophisticated ways of surviving which then become normal patterns of behaviour. It may be the child who has learned to be very quiet or very helpful or very loud to stop the adult from rejecting them altogether.

When children are growing up in these circumstances, having their senses on high alert becomes a normal state of being. As the brain is wired through relational experiences, their brains develop to see the world as a place full of risk and that adults are not predictable or safe. Brain development is largely dependent and responsive to our experience of the sensory world so smells sounds and visuals that have a resonance of a time of danger and alert the child stress management system to respond to danger. Children who experience toxic stress find it very hard to experience calmness, even when there is no obvious threat. They will respond to the world and all it offers in a very different way to children whose early life has been consistently safe and nurturing.

If we can see a child is in fight/flight/freeze, what are the immediate things we can do to help them?

Children's ability to keep calm and regulated is only developed alongside a regulated adult. The children's growing nervous system mirrors that of the adult they are with. Children's bodies only learn how to soothe themselves, stay calm, manage stress if they have had an adult co-regulating alongside them, for many children growing up in adverse experiences often do not have adults who have regulated nervous systems and are also experiencing high levels of stress. A settled nervous system is required to do all the high-level functioning that school and nursery require. Learning, playing, cooper-ating, social interaction, self-organising, having fun, are all everyday normal experiences for many children, but not those raised in traumatic situations. This is not their norm and requires a level of brain functioning that is not possible in a hypervigilant brain wired to high levels of threat.

As practitioners, what are the things we need to look for in a child that would suggest they are being affected by high levels of stress?

The immediate signs of children affected by toxic stress can be very obvi-ous, but not always. It could be the child who is always ready to run or fight. Who is fidgety and can't settle and whose nervous system isn't regulated enough to make friends. It can also be the child who is very quick to please and appease everyone.

We need to look at the survival areas of fight/flight/freeze, and think about how that manifests in children's presentations. With the fight response, we might be seeing a child who is easy to get agitated, uses aggressive lan-guage, or misreads facial cues, tone and voice – they can have a caged tiger sort of response. These children are more likely to have conflict in the play-ground or react to adults, misunderstanding and thinking that the adult is being critical when that was not intended. These children have a heightened sense of outward reaction.

Children in flight could be hiding in places, avoid going into places like the classroom; they may find it hard to get back into the building after being outside; they are the children, when they perceive pressure, they need to leave and get away.

Freeze is a spectrum: from the more severe, disassociate response, chil-dren may faint or become physically unwell, having a physiological reaction.

Others absence themselves to a more daydreaming response. Also on the spectrum is appease, which could be seen as the fourth survival strategy. These are the children whose safety is around appeasing the adults; it looks like they are really helpful and noticing what is needed around them. Another description is fawn: a lot of people from an early stage, when they are experiencing danger around them, they numb themselves down to incongruence – they develop an ability to not notice or make everything OK when things are not OK; they learn not to make a fuss.

Are there key things we can think about if we know a child we are working with has been affected by trauma?

When we work with children who are affected by trauma, we need to remember our starting point is they have been affected by negative experiences. We need to ask questions:

- ▶ *Is the child thriving?*
- ▶ *Are there areas where they are less able to settle?*
- ▶ *Can they build relationships?*
- ▶ *Where do they feel less confident?*
- ▶ *Are their body systems, nervous systems, cognitive systems, sensory systems out of balance?*

We need to help them by looking at ways to tweak the situation they are in. Turn the temperature down for them, so they are less likely to fight or flight and more able to sensory and socially manage. We know that trauma can have an impact on the whole of the system. We just need to notice and observe the child, take on board the distress they are feeling and lack of ability to engage in certain tasks, and adapt that task so that it is manageable for them.

In later chapters, I will be exploring lots of practical ideas about how we can turn the temperature down for children, as Nicky describes. Most of the work we do as a team is helping staff to find creative ways to meet the child's sensory needs and adapt the situation they are in to enable the child to be able to participate and thrive.

Window of tolerance

The term 'window of tolerance' was developed by Daniel Siegel (2020), to help us understand how the body and brain react to stress, anxiety and adversity. The idea behind it is that each person's window of tolerance is their own emotional state which helps them to manage and experience the normal daily life experiences of tiredness, pain, sadness and anger. Most of the time we stay within our window of tolerance – sometimes an experience will take us to the edge of our window, but we have developed a regulation system and we have tools and strategies that enable us to come back to balance. If we experience an extreme stress, that can move us out of the window and can lead to hyper-arousal (such as feeling anxious, panicky, restless, finding it hard to sleep) or hypo-arousal (for example, shutting down, exhaustion, shutting down depressed). When we are outside of the window of tolerance, we can flit between hyper-arousal and hypo-arousal. For children who have experienced trauma and adverse childhood experiences, their window of tolerance may be a lot narrower than a child who has had calm, stable and secure experiences. At the end of this chapter is a link to a YouTube clip about window of tolerance, made by a charity called Beacon House (2018). If the idea of window of tolerance is new to you, I would recommend stopping and watching this short film.

Being stuck

What we know from developmental psychology is that some children who experience ongoing toxic stress and trauma can become stuck at developmental stages. For example, the child who experienced a traumatic experience at the age of 2 may often go back to the behaviours of that age and stage when they are distressed. As children get older, we often hear adults becoming infuriated by children's behaviour and telling them to act their age, without understanding that there are many children whose body and mind are holding on to the negative experiences they have had. The body and mind can take them back to the age they were when these happened. In our team we use the Thrive approach (2021), which is a social and emotional developmental model that links child development theory with attachment theory and uses play and creativity to build trusting and safe relationships with adults. The Thrive approach helps us to consider the stages a child may have become stuck in. If you are unfamiliar with it, take a look at the Thrive website (see 'Further information and references').

Attachment

Many children who show signs of SEMH needs may also have some attachment difficulties. We know that a secure attachment to their parents, or main caregivers if these are not biological parents, is crucial for every child. The early work of John

Bowlby (1969), and then Mary Ainsworth's (1969) Strange Situation research, have been vital in the ongoing research into attachment theory. If this is a new area to you, Helen Barrett's (2005) article in *Nursery World* introduces John Bowlby and his theories, and you can find a clip showing Mary Ainsworth's Strange Situation on YouTube (2016). Our knowledge of attachment has grown over the years and we now have a greater understanding of the difficulties that occur when there are attachment difficulties. We also know that for many children their parents are not always able to offer a secure attachment. Daniel Siegel and Tina Payne Bryson, in *The Power of Showing Up* (2020), use a phrase called 'parental presence'. This describes parents who can reflect on and make sense of their own story of attachment and parenting, and this enables them to be able to physically and emotionally show up for their children. Children need parents who are present both physically and emotionally. It's not unusual for us to see parents who may be physically present but not emotionally present. How many times do we see parents who are in the same room but on their phone or other devices, not being able to give the children the attention or emotional support and input they need? Often the worry can be if an adult has not had a good attachment relationship in their childhood, then this is going to impact and affect the way they can be parents. What I love about Siegel and Payne Bryson's work, and also that of Nadine Burke Harris (2014, 2018), is their focus on how history does not have to dictate our future. They all describe how the problems adults may have had in their childhood can be worked through, and with attention and support we can choose to be different parents to our children. Siegel and Payne Bryson remind us that the behaviours needed for a secure attachment can be learned. There is hope.

A brief look at attachment

I am going to look briefly at attachment style, but if this area is to you I would suggest you do some further reading on this. Daniel Siegel is a good place to start – he has written several books (Siegel 2020; Siegel and Payne-Bryson 2020) and has many YouTube videos and podcasts you could listen to (see 'Further information and references').

Secure attachment

Children who have experienced secure attachment are those who have parents who are attuned to their child's needs and can meet those needs. They have parents who can soothe and comfort their child. They have parents who are mostly physically and emotionally present and available to the child. These are not perfect parents, but they are parents who can put the needs of the child first. These children believe they can trust their parents and adults who care for them – they know they are safe and loved.

Avoidant attachment

Children who have experienced avoidant attachment are those whose parents did not respond to their child's needs – for instance, they left them crying for extended periods, and were unable to understand the needs of the child (such as when it is a hungry cry or a cry of needing to be changed). They have dismissed the child's needs – for example, describing a child who is hungry and crying as being naughty or a nuisance – and been unable to offer the emotional support the child needed. With an avoidant attachment, the child doesn't expect to be cared for or to have their needs met. These children can sometimes get to the stage where they don't recognise their own needs, and they learn to not pay attention to their emotional feelings.

Ambivalent attachment

Children who have experienced ambivalent attachment are those whose parents are sometimes able to meet their needs – they will recognise the cry is one for hunger and will feed them. But at other times the parent's emotional needs are so high they are unable to recognise the need in the child and can ignore or be very stressed and anxious with the child – for instance, they pick up the hungry child, but feel panicky and stressed and are unable to think about feeding the child, and their high-stress levels are picked up on and experienced by the child. With an ambivalent attachment, the child never knows when their needs will be met, or what to expect. These children can sometimes get to the stage where they feel they cannot trust anyone, as they might be let down at any point.

Disorganised attachment

Children who have experienced disorganised attachment are those whose parents scare them. The child's repeated experience is that the parent is frightening, threatening or hugely neglectful. This can lead to a child feeling that life is very chaotic and overwhelming. With a disorganised attachment, the child lives in fear. They feel that the world and people around them are unsafe and frightening.

Children who have a secure attachment with their main caregivers can navigate their way through the world knowing that they are loved, feeling safe and able to try new things. Children with a secure attachment are generally resilient and able to cope with most of life's difficulties and failings. These children are ready to learn, to trust the adults around them and to make friends. Children who have had difficulties in their attachment can be in fear, untrusting of adults, and they may find it difficult to make friends. They may be anxious to try new things, they may find it difficult to concentrate and learn and they often find change overwhelming and frightening.

Moving between

Although there are clear attachment styles, the current thinking is that children with attachment difficulties experience several, if not all, elements of the styles. It is often more of a blended thing: you may find that children have more of a predominant aspect, but are more likely to experience elements of all the attachment styles. When I look back and reflect on the children I have worked with over the years, who have experienced attachment difficulties, I think all of them have shown elements of a variety of attachment styles.

What to do with this information

With all this knowledge of attachment, ACEs and trauma, we need to hold this information in mind when we work with and support children. As I mentioned in the introduction, sometimes Early Years practitioners are the first people to begin to consider whether a child has additional needs for which they need support. Of course, as Early Years practitioners, we are not the people to be diagnosing or jumping to conclusions, but we can start to gather pieces of the jigsaw together and begin to wonder, observe, ask questions about what might be going on for a child. It's important to hold these pieces of information in mind, as it will help us to plan and support the child.

Conclusion

In this chapter we have started to explore the term 'SEMH'. We have looked at ACEs, trauma and attachment, and its long-term impact, and considered how children can become stuck in early developmental stages. As I finish this chapter, I want to acknowledge that some of the children we work with are anxious – they are finding it hard to manage their emotions and feelings – and there is no obvious reason for it. I think it is important to note that not all children with SEMH needs have had a traumatic, neglectful or abusive past. It is significant that we note this, because we are increasingly aware and switched on to thinking about those children and what might be happening for them, but other children are showing signs of anxiety, struggling with their emotions and feelings, and they can get missed because they don't have the obvious indicators or known risk factors. As Early Years practitioners, we need to remain curious at all times, asking the question 'I wonder what the child is feeling/what they are trying to tell me.' Remembering that behaviour is always a form of communication.

 Further information and references

Barrett, H. (2005) Early Years Pioneers: John Bowlby. Available at www.nurseryworld.co.uk/features/article/early-years-pioneers-john-bowlby\

Barrett, W. (2018) Why I Worry About the ACE-Aware Movement's Impact. Available at www.tes.com/news/why-i-worry-about-ace-aware-movements-impact

Beacon House (2018) Resources: Animations – Window of Tolerance. https://beaconhouse.org.uk/resources/

Bombèr, L. (2020) *Know Me to Teach Me: Differentiated Discipline for Those Recovering from Adverse Childhood Experiences.* New York: Worth Publishing.

Bowlby J. (1969) *Attachment and Loss,* vol. 1, *Loss.* New York: Basic Books.

Burke Harris, N. (2014) How Childhood Trauma Affects Health Across a Lifetime. TEDMED2014, September. Available at www.ted.com/talks/nadine_burke_harris_how:childhood_trauma_affects_health_across_a_lifetime

Burke Harris, N. (2018) *The Deepest Well: Healing the Long-Term Effects of Childhood Adversity.* London: Bluebird.

Center on the Developing Child (2015) Take the ACE Quiz – And Learn What It Does and Doesn't Mean. Available at https://developingchild.h

arvard.edu/media-coverage/take-the-ace-quiz-and-learn-what-it-does -and-doesnt-mean/

Felitti, V. J. et al. (1998). Relationship of childhood abuse and household dysfunction to many of the leading causes of death in adults: The Adverse Childhood Experiences (ACE) Study. *American Journal of Preventive Medicine* 14(4), 245–258.

NHS Digital (2018) One in eight of five to 19-year-olds had a mental disorder in 2107 major new survey finds. Available at https://digital.nhs.uk/news -and-events/latest-news/one-in-eight-of-five-to-19-year-olds-had-a-m ental-disorder-in-2017-major-new-survey-finds

Public Health Scotland (2021) Adverse Childhood Experiences (ACEs). Available at www.healthscotland.scot/population-groups/children/adve rse-childhood-experiences-aces/should-services-ask-about-aces

Siegel, D. (2020) *The Developing Mind: How Relationships and the Brain Interact to Shape Who We Are*, 3rd edition. New York and London: Guilford Press.

Siegel, D. and Payne-Bryson, T. (2020) *The Power of Showing Up: How Parental Presence Shapes Who Our Kids Become and How Their Brains Get Wired*. London: Scribe.

Sunderland, M. (2016) *What Every Parent Needs to Know. Love, Nurture and Play with Your Child*. London: Dorling Kindersley.

Thrive (2021) The Thrive Approach. Available at www.thriveapproach.com

van der Kolk, B. (2014) *The Body Keeps the Score: Mind, Brain and Body in the Transformation of Trauma*. London. Penguin.

World Health Organization (2018) Adverse Childhood Experiences International Questionnaire (ACE-IQ). Available at www.who.int/violence _injury_prevention/violence/activities/adverse_childhood_experiences/en/

YouTube (2016) Mary Ainsworth's Strange Situation. Available at www .youtube.com/watch?v=9WyHo3jGx7k

2 Social, emotional and mental health needs in children

Part II: Exploring these needs in further detail

The aim of this chapter is to help you start thinking about the children who may be experiencing some additional social, emotional and mental health needs. Chapter 1 listed a few of the behaviours that you may see in children who are showing signs of having higher SEMH needs, and this chapter is going to look at these more closely.

The NICE (2008) guidance for schools describes social, emotional and mental health in children as:

▶ social: has good relationships with others and does not have behavioural difficulties
▶ emotional: is happy and confident and is not anxious or depressed
▶ psychological: is able to be autonomous, problem-solve, manage emotions, experience empathy, have resilience and be attentive.

In the team I work with, we support children who have been identified as needing additional support in the last term at nursery and in their Reception year. The Early Years settings are asked to make referrals, through the local authority, of children who they think will find the transition into school a challenge due to social, emotional and mental health reasons. We encourage Early Years settings to think about what some of the early identifying indicators could be that show a child may find the transition especially hard. We know that for all children the transition to school is a massive change, and it is one where we need to give all children support. However, children who have additional social, emotional and mental health needs can find a big change like this especially hard. I know that our service is very unusual and there may not be a similar service in your area, however, as Early Years staff it is still important for us to recognise and identify those children that we think may find changes particularly difficult, and put in extra support and resources for these children. We can then share ideas with the new school or staff in the new room about what helps the child. Additional support for a child doesn't need to mean extra staffing, but this is about thinking about the specific needs of the child and how we can meet them. Often this can be done with some flexible and creative thinking. Ideas for this will be shared throughout the book.

We encourage staff to think about what they know already and what they are seeing. The staff have a wealth of knowledge and insight, and sometimes we need to sit and reflect on what we know before we start to think about a plan for moving forward in supporting the child.

The following lists are to be used as reflective exercises. We created them for the Early Years settings in our area so they can be used to help them reflect on the children they are working with. They are not exhaustive lists, but are meant as prompts – some questions to use as a conversation starter in the team when reflecting on a child. We are not using the lists to diagnose a child; as Early Years workers, that is not our role. However, they can be useful to help us think about the children we are supporting and what they may or may not find difficult. Using this information can help to give us a fuller picture of the child and how we can support them. Remember: these are used by staff who work with children aged 3 or 4, in the year before they start school. The questions can still be useful with slightly younger children, but always consider the usual child development you would expect of the child at that age.

Behaviour questions

We ask these questions because often behaviour is one of the first areas professionals and parents start to talk about and notice that the child may be struggling. If this is an area a child finds difficult in their Early Years settings, it is likely they will continue to struggle with this as they go through their Early Years setting and into school, and they may need additional support.

1. *Does the child separate from parents/carers easily?* Many children find the initial separation very tricky and we would expect a child who is new to any setting to find the separation hard. Sometimes we see children where this goes on for a lot longer. If you have a child who finds this separation tricky, you could ask: *Is the child frequently distressed in your setting? Are they clingy to the adults?* You may have noticed that the child who finds separation from the

parents difficult is also a child who becomes distressed regularly, or needs to be by the side or in sight of their key worker all the time. However, the second question may be relevant to children who don't find the separation from carers hard, but are clingy to other adults.

2. *Does the child interact with other children in the way you would expect for their age and development?* As experienced Early Years practitioners, we know developmentally how children respond to other children and we also know the developmental-appropriate behaviours. Some of the children may not be showing these. For example, you may have a child who is 4 years old but is unable to play with other children. Instead, they play alongside other children, or they may not tolerate any other children in their space when they are playing. If you are unfamiliar with developmental stages of play, Kathy Brodie's (2018) book is a good place to start with this.

3. *Does the child appear withdrawn?* Some children almost seem to disappear. You don't notice them, they don't stand out to you as staff, they may often be quiet, they don't necessarily refuse to do things, but they don't actively engage, either. They may spend a lot of time standing and watching or be on the edge of the room quietly playing and watching.

4. *Does the child appear hypervigilant?* These are the children who appear to be engrossed in play but then notice and hear when someone new quietly enters the room. It may be the child who takes a long time to eat lunch, as they are constantly watching, aware of everything that is happening around them.

5. *Does the child show a lot of 'over-the-top' behaviours?* Some children are known by everyone: you arrive in the room and they may be the child that is loud, bouncy, running around the space; they may be the child that appears to be rougher in their play or the child whose name you often hear being mentioned by all the staff.

6. *Is the child affected by the behaviour of others?* A comment I often hear from staff or parents is '"Tom" will be fine as long as he is not with other children who encourage him to play up.' Some children appear to be easily drawn into certain behaviours by other children. On the flip side of this, some children become easily distressed by other children's behaviour.

7. *Does the child seem anxious?* Anxiety may show itself in different ways with young children. They may find the many changes in the day distressing, or be worried about a variety of things, such as going into the toilet or trying something new. One way they may show this is by being upset regularly, or they may be selective mute in the setting.

8. *Does the child show executive functioning?* This means, for example, thinking through and/or recalling from previous learning. Executive function often begins to develop around 3 to 5 years. A child whose executive function is developing can cope with being on a task without being easily distracted, they can make simple plans and choices, they can begin to think things through – for example, 'If I hit Peter, he will be sad.'

9. *Does the child engage in unwanted physical behaviour towards other children or adults?* Some children are regularly violent to other children or adults or both, hitting, punching, spitting, kicking, pulling hair, etc.

10. *How does the child cope with transitions?* This could be transitioning from one activity to another or stopping to go for lunch, for example. Some children find transitions very stressful and distressing. For example, they may become upset when they have to stop their play, or become dysregulated when they are told it is time to come inside.

Health questions

Some of these might seem a bit curious, but again it is not a judgemental list, but one to reflect upon. This list has arisen from some of the common health needs we have witnessed in the children we have worked with over the years.

1. *Was the child born at full term?* This question isn't always asked when a child starts nursery or school, but we feel it is important to ask this. If a child was born prematurely, we would then want to know how premature, whether they were in the special care baby unit and for how long? We know that if a child is born prematurely this can have an impact on their development.

2. *Has the child had one or more instances of glue ear while they have been attending nursery?* Children who regularly get glue ear can sometimes find it hard to concentrate, as it may impact their speech and language and ability to communicate, their ability to hear and follow instructions, etc. The NHS website (2020a) has some useful information on glue ear (see 'Further information and references').

3. *Does the child have motor difficulties (fine or gross)?* Think what you might expect an average child of that age to do with their motor skills – for example, can they throw a ball, pick up small things, etc.?

4. *Does the child have a sense of themselves in space?* For example, are they able to run across a room without barging into or across other children or

things? Some children appear to have no sense of their body in a spatial awareness sense. These are children who often bump into others unintentionally: they may fall over or bump into things that are in their space.

5. *Has the child had multiple teeth removed?* We are seeing a growing number of children who have had large numbers of their milk teeth removed. This can have an impact on eating and speaking.

6. *In your opinion, does the child get enough sleep?* When we start work with families, we always ask about the child's sleep: when they go bed, how much sleep they get, whether they are easy to wake up, if they wake several times in the night. Many of the children we work with have sleep problems. The NHS (2020b) website recommends that children between the ages of 2 and 5 years get 11 to 12 hours' sleep a night.

7. *Does the child eat well while at your setting?* Or are there any feeding issues you are aware of? It's not unusual for the children we support to have various difficulties around eating. This may be because they are very particular about the food they eat – the flavour or texture. Some children refuse to eat in the education setting, while others eat everything available and yet still say they are hungry all the time.

8. *Does the child have an age-appropriate vocabulary, and can you understand their speech?* We know that communication and language is a growing difficulty for many children, often the children we work with have communication difficulties. If a child is unable to communicate clearly, in a way that people around them can understand, this can be hugely frustrating for the child. The Communication Trust (2021) has a useful guidance sheet on children's communication and language development, including ideas on the sounds, words and understanding that children generally have at different ages (see 'Further information and references' at the end of the chapter).

9. *Does the child use language which shows that they understand basic emotional and physical states – for example, do they use words to show you that they are happy/sad/cross/hot/cold, etc.?* By the age of 3 or 4, we would expect a child to be aware of the words and feelings around happy, sad, cross, hurt, cold and hot. Some children use these words all the time, but others seem unaware of these feelings and, even if they hear the words around them, they don't use them.

10. *Does the child know if they are hot or cold?* Some children they have no idea about this. I once worked with a child who I thought had thrown water over his head, as he was dripping. It turned out it was sweat – he was so hot, he had his jumper on and had been running around, and he didn't know or notice he was hot.

11. *What kind of eye contact does the child make?* Some children find it very difficult to have eye contact. They may look away, look down or even physically move away when you try to get them to look at you. Sometimes this happens if a child feels they are in the wrong. But, for other children, this is something they always find hard.

12. *What stage of toileting development is the child at?* Most children will be out of nappies and dry during the day by the age of 3. Every year we have a few children we work with who are going to school in nappies. For children where this is an ongoing difficulty, the charity ERIC (2021) can offer guidance and support.

Play questions

For this section we recommend that staff use the Leuven Well-Being Scale (Plymouth City Council 2011; see 'Further information and references'), which helps to reflect on how the child plays. This is a useful scale, assisting us in our observations and helping us to assess how engaged the child is in their play and to reflect on their wellbeing.

1. *Does the child engage with play and play opportunities?* When you start observing some children, you realise they don't play – they may flit around the setting, moving quickly from play area to play area. And there are other children who sit and watch and then go up, say, to another child's tower, kick it down and then move away.

2. *Does the child play with other children or on their own?* Also consider if they are playing alongside or interactively. In the second behaviour question, about how children interact with others (see above), I mentioned the developmental stages of play (Brodie 2018). Some children find playing with other children very challenging – sometimes they just prefer being on their own. Others like the idea of playing with other children, but struggle to understand the social rules around turn-taking, listening to the ideas of others, etc. Yet other children can play alongside others but are unable to interact with others in their play – for instance, they almost appear in their own little world, not engaging in the play around them.

3. *Does the child use repetitive play?* Some children's play is very limited. They may play with the same toy or the same game again, and again, and again. This isn't unusual for short periods with some children, but it is something to think about if it goes on for an extended length of time.

4. *Does the child show joy in play?* The Leuven Well-Being Scale (Plymouth City Council 2011) is particularly useful for thinking about this.

Family questions

These questions are very similar to the ten areas looked at in ACEs, such as emotional abuse, physical abuse and domestic violence.

1. *Does the child have parents who engage in some form of violence (physical/ emotional or coercive) towards one another?*
2. *Are the child's parents living in the same house?* If the parents live in separate houses, another question would be, *If the child sees both parents, how much time is spent with both of them?*
3. *Does the family live in temporary accommodation or have they ever been homeless?* If they are in temporary accommodation, another question would be, *How many times have they moved and was this planned or sudden?*
4. *Is one of the child's parents in prison, or have they been to prison in the child's lifetime?* If a parent is currently in prison, another question would be, *Does the child have contact with, and visit, the parent?*
5. *Do either of the child's parents experience mental health difficulties, including depression?* If they do, another question would be if the parent has support for this, such as from mental health services.
6. *Do the child's parents/carers use drugs or alcohol, or have they in the child's lifetime?* If they do another question would be, *Are they having support from drug and alcohol services?*
7. *Does the child live with their birth parents?* If not, who does the child live with? If the child doesn't live with their birth parents, other questions would be, *When did the child stop living with the birth parents? How many different carers have they lived with? Do they still have contact with their birth parents?*

As I said at the beginning of these four sets of questions, they are not intended to be lists for diagnosing a child with additional SEMH needs. However, we can use them as a reflective exercise, helping us to think about and understand the lived story and experience of a child. In our experience, children who 'tick' several items on the lists are likely to find changes (such as moving rooms in the nursery, moving to school, having a new sibling) incredibly stressful and frightening, and can easily become overwhelmed. As Early Years professionals, having this type of information to hand can help us to think and plan ahead, and to recognise that we will need to put in additional support, especially at times of change.

There are some children we work with where we are not surprised, as Early Years professionals, that they may show signs of distress at big changes. However, there are other children who show us in different ways that they feel uneasy and find change hard, but these are less obvious.

TAKE A MOMENT

I encourage you to take a moment now to think about the questions. Is there a particular child that comes to mind when you go through them? If so, perhaps take note of this and share your thoughts with your team. Maybe do some more reflecting and thinking.

Below are two case studies of children who may be showing signs of needing additional support for their social and emotional and mental health. Their names have been changed.

CASE EXAMPLES

Lucy

Lucy is 3, and lives with Mum, Dad and five brothers and sisters. She is number three in the siblings, with twin brothers who are 1 year old. Mum had postnatal depression after Lucy and the twins' birth. The family lives in a three-bedroom housing association house on the edge of a village. There is domestic violence in one of the neighbouring houses, which the family can hear, loudly, through the wall. The other next-door neighbour is a suspected drug dealer. Dad is a dairy farmer and works on a nearby farm, while Mum works evenings at the local pub. The family would like to move, but the house is convenient for Dad's work.

Lucy attends the local pre-school attached to the village school, and has been going there since she was 2 years, 6 months. She attends three days a week. Lucy is quiet and withdrawn when at pre-school, and still finds it very hard to leave Mum, often crying for at least half an hour when she leaves. Lucy has some communication difficulties. Her parents can understand what she is saying, but the pre-school staff find it difficult to understand all that she says. Lucy often stands and watches, although if staff support her she will sometimes join in with a bigger group. She often has a fixed smile on her face and, when you ask her how she feels, she always says happy. However, her eyes tell a different story – they are lacking a sparkle. Lucy has not made friends, and mostly plays by herself – she is easily upset by other children's boisterous or noisy play. Lucy loves the farm animals and will mostly play with these or the water tray. She is often very tired and still needs an afternoon nap. Lucy will be starting school in three months and, although school is on the same site as the pre-school, Mum and the pre-school staff are worried how Lucy will manage the transition. They are particularly concerned that Lucy will find full-time school too much.

Ozzie

Ozzie is 4 years old. He lives with Mum and one younger brother. When Ozzie was 2, the family lost their home and were in temporary hostel accommodation for six months. When the family was rehoused, Mum and Dad split up. Ozzie attends nursery four days a week, and has been in the nursery since he was 9 months old. Over the last six months, Ozzie has become increasingly violent: he regularly flies into a rage and hurts other children and adults. He hates change and will become very angry if his routine is altered. Ozzie is extremely energetic in the nursery. He prefers being in the garden to being inside, and also favours construction kits over imaginative play. Most other children are now afraid of Ozzie, which makes him sad, and he struggles to understand why they won't play with him. When children do play with him, he has to be in charge and will get very cross if they don't do what he wants.

Questions re case studies

▶ As an Early Years setting, what support could you put in place for both Lucy and Ozzie?
▶ The transition to school will be a challenge for Lucy and Ozzie and their families. What extra support could you provide?
▶ What information can you share with the school as part of the transition process?

These two children have very different needs, but they are both going to need additional support as part of their transition into school. Lucy is the type of child who could quite easily go under the radar – it's not unusual for the quiet, withdrawn children to be overlooked as needing additional support. However, with Ozzie it is likely to be recognised that the move to school is going to be hard and overwhelming for him. Chapter 6 focuses on the subject of transitions, and offers ideas for ways to support children with SEMH needs in their transitions.

 Interview with Ruth Fergusson

Ruth manages our team and is a senior education psychologist. This interview with Ruth helps us consider how we can support children we feel could benefit from additional support.

If an Early Years setting has been through the questions we use, and they have identified one of the children experiences several of the things on their list, can you suggest some simple ways the setting can support the child?

I would check staff were clear about the impact of early family experiences on children's development. I would check they had a good understanding about the chances of the child being stuck in certain developmental stages, depending on the timing of the experience the child had. If the child's life experience from birth had been one of consistent upheaval, then the behaviours they were seeing may be indicative of much earlier childhood behaviours. I would explore with staff what the behaviour was indicating – not just that it was something they needed to manage; we would explore what we know from developmental psychology around what the behaviour was likely to be, say, stuck or unlevelled stages of development. Then we would think about what we know makes the difference for children – things like predictability, consistency and routine.

To help staff think about this, I would then get them to break down each part of the day.

> *From the moment the child appears, how the child and carer expect that to be, who is the named key worker to meet and greet the parent and child, are they always there? If they are not going to be there, I would encourage thinking about how that information was shared with the family at home.*

▶ *How the child is handed over, how they respond to the key person.*

▶ *How the child presents when the child arrives at school. Was the separation difficult? Did the child come in wound up and need calming? Or did they find it difficult to separate? Does that separation need elongating and the parent comes in for 10 minutes, or do you agree to go out to the gate to meet the child and you do a calming exercise across the playground as you get into the building?*

I would then want to know in detail where the pinch points were through the day. What is tricky? Is it around transition? How do we ease those? Do they need to be done separately? Does someone always need to have eyes on the child at every transition – for example, between activities, going to the toilet, getting the toys out, etc.?

We recommend using the Leuven scale. Can you explain how that can be helpful?

I would encourage settings to look at and use the Leuven scales. Get three people at three different times on three different days to use the Leuven scale – it doesn't need to take long. Then sit down as a team and review what you have, see where the tricky points are. Is one day worse than another? Spot patterns in the child's behavior. Have the strapline 'This is communication, this isn't something we can't deal with, it's a communication that someone isn't feeling happy.'

Sometimes settings can feel overwhelmed by what they are seeing and hearing. What could help with this?

Sometimes it can be easy to get into the catastrophising and thinking 'What can we possibly do, it's so terrible at home?' We need to see this is just one person's life experience, it isn't unmanageable. With children, this happens in relationships. It's empowering everyone to see that relationships are the venue for change, and if we get the relationship right, then we see change happen. When we feel overwhelmed or have catastrophised, or we feel it is an enormous thing that we can't manage, then we are already inhibiting the power of the relationship we can have with that child. Whereas, if we can say, 'OK, this a communication and I might not get it right every time, but I understand you are trying to tell me something and I can see this is not OK for you at the moment,' once we start to start to see it in that way, then it feels more manageable, and we can start to put things in place that we know help – routine, consistency, predictability, increasing or reducing sensory experiences. Put those in place; also look at what are the relationships like with other children, how included do they feel, how can you bring other children into that child's world so they feel part of something.

Sometimes this is as much to do with how the staff feels about their own agency: if staff feel blocked by their capacity to do it, then they won't try and do it. We need managers to set a tone about how we feel confident and able to work with these children, and avoid the groupthink of things that are awful and won't change.

What to do next

If you have used the questions in this chapter and are working with a child who shows several of the needs, there are a few actions you can take (along taking on board Ruth's thoughts above).

- ▶ In supervision, discuss the child and your concerns.
- ▶ As a team, think about what you are all seeing. Reflect on what is working and not working.
- ▶ Have a conversation with parents. Ask how things are at home generally, and what the child's behaviour is like. Do the parents have concerns?
- ▶ Use the Leuven scale to help you think about when the child is showing high signs of wellbeing, and when they are not.
- ▶ After making adjustments around additional support for transitions, extra warnings of changes, considerations around the beginning and end of the day, you may find you still need some additional ideas and support. Have a conversation with the child's health visitor. If you have an area SENCO in your local authority, or an Early Years team of advisory teachers, contact them for support and advice, and make sure you alert the school about your thinking.

Conclusion

Hopefully, the questions in this chapter will have helped you think about some of the children you work with. I know it can be really easy to fall into negative thinking around certain children, and have a feeling of hopelessness and 'stuckness'. I often see and hear this in nurseries in the sixth term, when staff feel totally exhausted and the story and experience around the child have become huge and negative. It is so key to have good supervision sessions where staff can talk through concerns, key persons know they have the support of managers, and teams are able to work together to think through what the child is trying to communicate to us. My hope is that the lists of questions may help you to open up some of the conversations and reflections around the children you work with and maybe find puzzling or challenging.

 Further information and references

Brodie, K. (2018) *The Holistic Care and Development of Children from Birth to Three: An Essential Guide for Practitioners and Parents.* Abingdon: Routledge.

The Communication Trust/UCL Institute of Education (2021) How Children Develop Speech, Language and Communication Skills. Available at www .thecommunicationtrust.org.uk/media/600981/ite_resource_1.pdf

ERIC (2021) ERIC: The Children's Bowel & Bladder Charity. Available at www.eric.org.uk

NHS (2020a) Glue Ear. Available at www.nhs.uk/conditions/glue-ear/

NHS (2020b) How Much Sleep Do Children Need? Sleep and Tiredness. www.nhs.uk/live-well/sleep-and-tiredness/how-much-sleep-do-kids-need/

NICE (2008) Social and Emotional Wellbeing in Primary Education. www.nice.org.uk/guidance/ph12/resources/social-and-emotional-wellbeing-in-primary-education-pdf-1996173182149

Plymouth City Council (2011) Observing Learning, Playing and Interacting in the EYFS: Leuven Well Being and Involvement Scales. Available at www .plymouth.gov.uk/documents-ldtoolkitleuven.pdf

Social, emotional and mental health needs in children

Part III: Exploring domestic violence, foetal alcohol syndrome, parental mental illness and children who are fostered or adopted

In this chapter, we are going to look in more detail at some of the life difficulties that children experience, and how this can have an impact on their social, emotional, and mental health. I am going to look in more detail at domestic violence, foetal alcohol syndrome, parental mental illness and on children who have been fostered and adopted. These subjects are heavy, as I have mentioned in earlier chapters, so please take care of yourself while you read this. If this feels too much today, you might wish to skip this chapter, move on to another one, and come back to this one later.

Domestic violence

At the time of writing (March 2021), the Social Care Institute for Excellence (2021) website suggests that in the UK one in seven children and young people under the age of 18 will have lived with domestic violence (Women's Aid 2021) at some point in their childhood. We are currently still in lockdown for Covid-19, and there have been growing reports and concerns around the increase of domestic violence during this time. For some, home is not a safe place to be, particularly during the time of lockdown. The charity Refuge (2020) reported from the beginning of lockdown they had a 25 per cent increase in calls to their helpline, and visits to their website increased by 150 per cent. At the point you are reading this book, the initial statistic I have shared is likely to be higher. Hopefully, this life will have become more normal, with a return to Early Years settings and workplaces, but the number of families where there has been violence during lockdown will have increased. The repercussions of this will go on for a long period.

Kate Brown, writing for the Crown Prosecution Service (2021), says:

> Domestic abuse, or domestic violence, is defined across Government as any incident of controlling, coercive or threatening behaviour, violence or abuse between those aged 16 or over who are or have been intimate partners or family members, regardless of their gender or sexuality.

Children who live in households where there is domestic violence may witness this in various ways:

- They may see the violence, they may be in the same room or they may get caught up in the middle of the violent act.
- They may be in a different room, but hear the violence or see injuries caused by a violent act or broken objects after the act.
- They may hear verbal violence and may be encouraged to join in or take sides.

Some parents believe that children are unaware of the violence, reporting that they were in bed, too young and/or not at home. Evidence shows children are often more aware of the violence than their parents believe. Many children who have lived in households with domestic violence will describe vividly what was happening (Sterne and Poole 2010).

These are the impacts of domestic violence on children's wellbeing and mental health:

- Children's sleep may be affected, by being woken up by arguments or the sounds of violence.
- Children may become hurt (physically and emotionally) in trying to protect the person from being abused.
- Children may become anxious and scared.
- Children may be reluctant to leave the family home or leave the parent that is being abused.
- Children may become hypervigilant, impacting their ability to concentrate and learn.
- Children may become violent or aggressive to the parent/other adults or children.
- If the abuser is controlling, there may be limited availability to food/going outside/seeing others or getting medical support.

▶ Children may be constantly in fear of what they are going home to and/or what might happen next.

Domestic violence and under-5s

It is not unusual for domestic violence to begin during pregnancy. The effects in pregnancy and early life of a child can include (Sterne and Poole 2010):

▶ death of baby due to premature labour/miscarriage
▶ poor growth of the baby in the uterus, leading to an impact on brain development
▶ difficulties in developing a secure attachment
▶ eating difficulties which could lead to failure to thrive
▶ behaviour difficulties, such as violent outbursts, very distressing behaviours, extreme startle response, or withdrawn and passive or frozen response.
▶ emotional difficulties – for example, often distressed, crying a lot, nervous, clingy, fearful
▶ difficulties in socialising with peers
▶ delay in development, including language development, toileting development, play skills
▶ difficulty in managing change and transitions
▶ sleep issues: struggling to go to sleep/waking regularly/nightmares

We know from earlier chapters that, if a child has experienced the trauma of living with domestic violence, this will have an impact on their brain development, their stress levels and their ability to function. These are long-lasting impacts and will last beyond the immediate time the child lived with the trauma.

You may know of a family who is experiencing domestic violence, which may be information that has already been shared with the setting. Or you may have suspicions that this might be so. It is important for Early Years settings to know where to signpost families locally for help, to know the charities available nearby or local authority provision. Also, health visitors and or the local children centre (if you still have these in your area) will be able to offer support. It's important that families know they are not being judged about their situation, but that you can direct them towards support.

Domestic violence can be such a difficult subject to talk about – there is still so much shame around this subject. If this is a new area for you, I would encourage you to do some further reading and take a look at the websites for domestic violence charities (both national and local). The Women's Aid website is very useful; Refuge also has an excellent website and a Freefone helpline. Remember that men can also be victims of domestic violence; there is a website specifically for men called Respect Men's Advice Line (which also has a Freefone helpline; also see 'Further information and references').

TAKE A MOMENT

Looking at the figures above, the number of children who have lived in domestic violent households is very high. Although domestic violence is now talked about more, in my experience it is still one of those areas where nursery workers and teachers have limited understanding. If you have limited knowledge of domestic violence in your team, I would recommend having a team meeting or a small training session around the subject. Enable the whole team to understand it a little more and help everyone to know what to look out for. Domestic violence charities have information sheets and sometimes films, or you may want to contact a local charity, to see if they can speak with your team.

Foetal alcohol syndrome

The guidance in the UK is not to drink alcohol in pregnancy, as we know that it passes through the placenta directly to the foetus and can cause abnormalities and affect foetal development. The alcohol passes through the mother's bloodstream directly to the foetus and, because it does not have a fully developed liver, is unable to filter out the toxins from the alcohol. The alcohol can harm the foetus's brain cells and damage its nervous system (National Organisation for FASD 2021).

Therefore, if the mother drinks heavily during pregnancy, this can cause harm to the baby and sometimes results in foetal alcohol syndrome. The National Organisation for Foetal Alcohol Syndrome Disorder (FASD; 2021) describes it as a 'neurodevelopmental condition with lifelong cognitive, emotional and behavioural challenges'.

Symptoms of FASD can include facial abnormalities. This does not always occur: some suggest that it occurs in around 10 per cent of children with FASD, as it only occurs if the mother was drinking heavily at the beginning of the pregnancy (when the face is forming). The characteristic features are:

▸ small eyes
▸ smaller head
▸ thin upper lip
▸ the smooth area between the nose and upper lip.

According to Brown and Mather (2014), facial issues are only obvious at birth in the most severely affected children. In other children it becomes more obvious between 8 months and 8 years of age, with them becoming less pronounced as they reach adolescence.

Other symptoms can include:

▸ poor growth
▸ movement and balance difficulties
▸ learning difficulties – such as thinking, speech, social skills, timekeeping, memory
▸ difficulties with attention and concentration
▸ hyperactivity
▸ aggression
▸ difficulties assessing risk
▸ mental health difficulties
▸ problems with liver, kidneys, heart or other organs
▸ hearing and sight difficulties.

The main difficulty related to foetal alcohol syndrome is often considered to be the long-term difficulties with learning, language and behaviour, which often become more apparent as the child is in nursery and then starts school. Difficulties around attention, following instructions and hyperactivity can begin to become more noticeable at this age.

FASD is often not diagnosed at birth, but as the child develops more questions can occur. However, it is not uncommon for children and adolescents with FASD to have multiple diagnoses and may not have a specific diagnosis for FASD. The

NHS Surrey and Borders Partnership Foundation Trust (2021) is the only specialist NHS clinic for FASD in the UK.

Researchers from the University of Bristol and Cardiff have been researching information about mothers drinking during pregnancy and the development of children, using the Bristol Children of the 90s study (13,495 children). They found that up to 79 per cent of children in the sample were exposed to alcohol in pregnancy and up to 17 per cent screened positive for FASD. The screening tool they used is not the same as a formal diagnosis. However, it indicates how much of a public health concern this should be (University of Bristol 2018).

As Early Years practitioners, we are not in the position to be making this diagnosis, but we need to be aware of children who may have been impacted by their mother drinking alcohol during pregnancy. For more information on this, I would suggest you look at the National Organisation for FASD website (see 'Further information and references'). If this is something that may be a difficulty for a child you are working with, I encourage you to have a conversation with their health visitor and share your thoughts, concerns and questions.

Parental mental health difficulties

We are increasingly aware of mental health difficulties and, although mental illness is no longer the taboo subject it once was, it still has a stigma attached for some people.

I feel I should start this section by announcing that parental mental health difficulties are a subject I have had a lot of personal experience with, as my mum has bipolar disorder. She was diagnosed (it was called manic depression back then) when I was born, and when I was growing up this was not openly discussed. Unfortunately, my mum spent a lot of time (at least twice a year, for a few months) in a psychiatric hospital. This is back in the 1970s and 1980s, and thankfully times have changed: many people with a mental health difficulty are now treated at home and psychiatric hospital admissions are a rare form of treatment, rather than the norm. However, although mental health is much more recognised, accepted and discussed openly – many books are now written on the subject, too – there is no doubt that for some people/families it can still feel taboo.

As Early Years practitioners, we need to be aware how mental health difficulties can have an impact on the family. One of the ACE categories is parental mental health difficulties, so we know it can be significant. Note: just because a parent has a mental illness, this does not automatically suggest they are unable to care for their children, but it may make their role as parents much harder, just as getting through every day when you feel mentally ill can feel so much more difficult.

Mental health difficulties can cover a variety of mental health conditions, including:

▶ depression
▶ anxiety disorder
▶ schizophrenia
▶ bipolar disorder
▶ personality disorder.

With all these illnesses, the experiences will be hugely varied for people. Some people with a diagnosed mental illness will find that life is mostly not impacted; they can successfully manage the condition on medication or with other forms of support. For other people, they may have acute periods of mental illness which have a huge impact on their own and the family's lives, yet for others it may have an underlying constant (but not huge) effect. This will all vary on the individual, their situations and the support they have.

At times, mental illness can occur alongside other stressful and life difficulties, such as (NSPCC 2021):

▶ divorce or separation
▶ unemployment
▶ financial hardship
▶ problems with housing
▶ discrimination.
▶ lack of social support.

I would also add 'world pandemics' to this list. As mentioned earlier, I am writing this book at the time of the Covid-19 lockdown, and there are increasing concerns about the impact the pandemic is having on people's mental health. Psychiatrists and psychologists in the UK were warning about the profound effect the pandemic was having on people's mental health and were predicting this would not just end when the lockdown ended. Hopefully, by the time you are reading this, the lockdown period will be a memory, but if the psychologists and psychiatrists are right it will have consequences on adults and children's mental health, running for years to come (Roxby 2020).

Sometimes a parent's mental illness can impact on how they parent:

▶ They may have difficulty in controlling their emotions in front of the children – for example, showing extreme sadness or anger or being overly happy, which can be described as manic episodes.

▶ They may have rapid mood swings, from very high to very low. This can be frightening and confusing to children.

▶ They may be withdrawn, emotionally unavailable.

▶ They may have high emotional needs, which they look to their children to meet. Or they look to their children for comfort or solace, putting a huge demand on children, leaving them feeling responsible for their parent's wellbeing.

▶ They are unable to recognise or meet their children's emotional needs.

▶ They may struggle to set boundaries.

▶ They may struggle to put in place routines – for example, mealtimes, bedtimes, getting their children to school or nursery.

▶ They may struggle to care for themselves and their children physically.

▶ They may find it hard to get out of bed and take care of their children.

▶ They may find it hard to shop, clean and cook.

▶ They may find it hard to work and earn money, and/or to pay bills.

▶ In worse cases, this can lead to neglect and abuse.

If a child lives with a parent who has a mental illness, this may impact the children. For example (NSPCC 2021):

▶ Children can take on a caring role with the parent and siblings, both emotionally and physically – for example, getting food, doing chores in the house.

▶ Children may feel responsible for their parent's illness.

▶ Children may feel responsible for trying to get their parent better.

▶ Children may feel constantly worried and scared about their parent's health.

▶ Children may feel fearful about what might happen or what their parent may do – they may have experienced or witnessed a frightening situation with their parent.

▶ Children may be isolated from others, or they may be worried about talking about their parent's health and behaviour to others (NSPCC).

The impacts on a child in the Early Years setting might include:

▶ The child may find it hard to concentrate.
▶ A child may be worried and fearful.
▶ The child may be anxious at leaving the parent or returning to them.
▶ The child may be hungry or dirty.
▶ The child may be concerned about the lack of food at home or clothes becoming dirty and needing washing.
▶ The child may be hypervigilant.
▶ The child may take on a caring role to others.
▶ The child may be lethargic.
▶ The child may be angry.

It is so helpful if a family informs us about mental illness. Then we can then be aware and support the family, ensuring that they know we are not judging them. It can become tricky when we think there may be mental health difficulties but the family has not spoken about the issue. Of course, if you have safeguarding concerns then you need to follow your procedures. However, if your concerns are not safeguarding but you are worried about the parent's mental health, have a conversation with the family. Check how they are, and ask if everything is OK. You could also speak with their health visitor. It is also important for you to be aware of local support that you can signpost families to. Mind, the national mental health charity, has offices and groups in most areas (see 'Further information and references').

TAKE A MOMENT

Although mental health is now talked about more openly in society, I would suggest that you to take a moment and consider how it is viewed in your workplace and/or family. This might be difficult. Is it OK if someone in your workplace says they are feeling anxious or depressed? Does your workplace signpost places of support for mental health? If it doesn't, I would urge you to look into this. There are some links at the end of the chapter. Chapter 12 explores adult wellbeing and offers some suggestions for supporting physical and mental health.

Fostered and adopted children

Children who are in foster care, have a special guardian or have been adopted will almost always have experienced trauma and loss. Even if a child was removed from their birth parents once born, they are likely to have experienced trauma in the womb. Decisions to have a child fostered, placed in special guardianship or adopted are not taken lightly in the UK, and almost always involve lengthy decision-making processes that include social workers, other professionals and the courts. A special guardian is someone with a close relationship with the child, such as a family member or close family friend. It is agreed, through court order, that they will be the permanent carer of the child.

In the United Kingdom, the number of children being fostered is rising: at the end of March 2019, 78,150 children were in the care of the local authority, an increase of 4 per cent on the previous year. At the same time, 3,570 looked after children were adopted and 7,130 were awaiting adoption (Coram BAAF 2021). Two years on, it is likely these figures will be higher again.

If a child in your setting is in foster care, special guardianship or has been adopted, as an Early Years worker you may not know the reason for the removal from the family home, and in many ways we don't need to know the details. However, you do need to have a trauma-informed practice in your mind. Even if a child cannot remember the traumas they have experienced, it is important for you to remember that the memory of these will reside in their bodies and stress systems. Bessel van der Kolk (2014) describes in great detail how the body holds on to the memory of trauma. As we explored in Chapter 1, if a child has no experience of safety and/or loving relationships, this will have affected their development. Dan Hughes (2012) describes how these children are highly likely to show dysregulated, impulsive behaviours. They can also be either rigid in their thinking and behaviour or chaotic.

It is recognised that looked after children are some of the most vulnerable children that we work with, and for this reason there is special legislation through the Children Act (1989) to ensure their additional needs are being met. Every local authority in England will have a virtual school for their looked after children, which will include a headteacher and teachers who oversee nursery, primary and secondary education. The virtual school's role is to make sure that the children have every opportunity to meet their full potential, and acts as the educational advocate on behalf of the child. They are involved in reviewing the education the child is receiving, making suggestions on support the child should be getting and advising on the setting they are to attend. In my experience of our local virtual school, they are a fantastic service to work with. They can: make sure the setting is offering the assistance they need to support the child; access other professionals to support the child and advise the setting; and get to know the child, their needs and interests, and ensure these are listened to and taken into consideration in the education setting. The virtual school teacher will oversee the looked after child's personal education plan (PEP) (Department for Education 2018).

Hopefully, the looked after and adopted children in your setting are now in a safe, secure and settled home. However, there are still times when fostered children have to move placement, which can happen for many different reasons. The hope is to keep them in a stable placement, but these can and do break down. I have worked with several children whose placements have become unsuccessful and where they have had numerous placements in a year. For all looked after and adopted children, the experience of moving families is traumatic and, the more times it happens, the more trauma this causes, on top of the initial trauma they experienced with their birth family. As I have mentioned in previous chapters, this will impact the child. For example, the child may:

▶ find transitions (big and small) very challenging
▶ struggle to concentrate
▶ have a delay in learning
▶ find it hard to trust adults
▶ be very controlling
▶ be anxious
▶ easily become dysregulated
▶ be fearful
▶ become very angry
▶ become withdrawn.

If you have a child who is looked after or has been adopted, even if the child appears to be OK, I would always presume that you will need to give them additional support when they are about to experience a big transition or change. I have worked with several adopted children, where they were with a new loving family, the child appeared happy in the nursery and there were no big concerns, and therefore no additional support was offered to the child on the move to school. The transition to school triggered a major reaction in the child – they were suddenly thrown into panic and rage and a sense of feeling very unsafe. This came as a complete surprise to the family, nursery and school. Always presume that a transition, such as a school, class or staff change, will be a potential threat to an adopted or fostered child. Louise Michelle Bombèr has written some fantastic books on how to support our most vulnerable children in school. Although they are not specifically aimed at Early Years practitioners, they contain some excellent ideas and wisdom that *are* relevant. Her most recent, *Know Me to Teach Me* (2020), contains lots of useful ideas and suggestions that apply to all ages.

Interview with Fred Lacey-Ford

Fred is a member of our team, and he and his partner adopted three children. Fred is a play therapist and a dyadic developmental psychotherapist. In this interview, he helps us to think about how we support looked after children.

If any Early Years setting has a looked after or adopted child in their setting, what are the key things they need to think about in supporting them?

My first suggestion would be to start with finding out if the child is formally looked after through social services. If they are, then as a setting make sure they are getting the right funding. The right funding is the pupil premium plus funding; this is for any education setting.

My second suggestion is to try and engage with the carers. Try and form a relationship with them. Relationships are unbelievably important; having children like this is incredibly isolating. Once you have gained the carer's trust, I think it is important for the family to feel they can share the child's story. Schools and nurseries need to be able to understand some of the issues the children have been facing. The reason I think this is, the education setting can then be prepared and understand certain behaviours. This is not about stigmatising children, it is about ensuring the best information and support is there for the family and children if difficulties occur. If something happens re certain behaviours, the education setting need to be able to step in, communicate with parents, and seek the right support. Families don't need to be sharing a detailed explanation, but they do need to share the headline. One of the core principles for me is the education setting needs to be invested in the child; when they are invested in a child we see those settings doing everything they possibly can for the child. By knowing something about the child, this can help the adults to be invested in the child.

My third suggestion is linked to relationships. We need to focus on social feedback. With children who have developmental trauma or attachment issues, they need as many positive messages from as many people as possible. If they get positive social feedback, from trusted adults in their education place throughout the day, from people who think they are amazing, then the children are much more likely over time to believe or trust in those messages. Whereas, if the children keep getting the repeated message of 'You're bad, you are not wanted here', then they believe that. Children need to have positive relationships with key adults outside of their family – this is wonderful for them.

My fourth suggestion is in the area of play and relationships with other children. Children who have had difficult starts in life often need someone alongside them structuring play and structuring the relationships with others. If children don't know what that looks like, we have to teach them. They need someone actively doing this with them; if you have a trusted person in the education setting who loves the child and is showing all that warmth and is supporting them, then you have children who are much more accepting and enriched by the activities and what you are getting them to do. We need to understand the child is often feeling very scared – their internal dialogue is 'This doesn't feel safe or this is scary', and so they refuse to engage. So as the adult, you need to create that safety for them by co-adventuring with them, so they know what that feels like. It has to be an active thing. It is not going to happen through osmosis; it has to actively take place.

My fifth suggestion is, it is important not to make over-allowances for the child, meaning the child is indulged or doesn't have the high expectations that you have for other children. Sometimes, some settings can hear the child's past story and then feel so sorry for them, they make allowances. That doesn't help the child. Adopted and looked after children need tighter boundaries around things, creating clear structure and clear expectations of what a child needs to do. This is so important; there is no harm in doing this. We need to see it as a two-hand model: with one hand we give with lots of positive regards, positivity, focus and attention; and in the other hand we are clear and say, 'That is not OK. I love you, but that behaviour is not acceptable.' It is the Dan Hughes model of 'I love you, I don't like that behaviour, it is not OK.' Boundaries are so important.

My sixth suggestion is around being sensitive about the difference. Education settings need to be aware that they might upset children if you do certain things – for example, if schools do family trees, work about grandparents or things about their history from birth. Education settings can often get this wrong; there are subtly different ways to do that which means you don't draw attention to the fact that children didn't always live with their parents. Be aware of the difference and open to difference as much you can. It doesn't take much, but it can make such a difference to a child and family.

My last suggestion is linked to the connection with parents. One of the most successful years we had for our youngest child was when one of his teachers met with us every six weeks to review and talk about how things were in school and at home. That made a massive difference in our relationship to the teacher and helped us to trust him. It made a difference to our child because he knew he was being kept in mind by all of us and it helped him feel safe. It was reassuring to us as parents. All it took was 10 minutes every six weeks; those 10 minutes made a huge difference.

Some children will need to play therapy to support them. Can you explain why play therapy can be beneficial?

Play therapy can work with any age child/ I have seen incredibly successful play therapy with children age 2 or 3. You need to create clear boundaries around the work. You usually have to adapt the work with younger children, so they would be shorter sessions. Play therapy is trying to enter into the world of the child and be there with them to support them, and you do it through play. If you are a Thrive practitioner and you play with a child through a sand tray or something similar, what you are doing is witnessing their play, you are sitting and watching and allowing them to express themselves through play. If you are doing play therapy, it is not the same. You are, in subtle and intricate ways, trying to understand the inner world of the child, and you do that with them, to sit there in that world with them, however that looks, whether it looks horrifying or if they express some abuse they have witnessed or whether they are joyful about something. Whatever it is, you are alongside them and you are feeling what they are feeling. Doing supervision work with play therapists, my lightbulb moment is often when they say, 'I felt so sad after that session, I don't know what that was about.' At that point, we explore and we say, 'OK, there was a good chance you were feeling so sad because the child was feeling so sad. There is a good chance you have pure transference of feeling from the child to you because they are sharing their inner world with you and sharing their inner feelings with you. You are honouring that by being with them and understanding that with them.' Can it be useful, absolutely, as children need someone to understand their inner worlds. Play therapy can provide that – not because it is making them better, but if you can sit with someone and understand what is going on for them, it can help, because you are sharing and they are not so alone with those feelings.

Conclusion

This chapter has explored in greater detail some key areas that some of the children we work with may have gone through. There are, of course, many different challenging experiences for the children we work with. However, I chose these areas to look at in more detail, as many of the children I have worked with encountered them.

Children who have gone through any of these (or other) difficulties need to know that in their Early Years setting they are safe and secure, and that the adults are there to protect, love, nurture and support them. Consistent routine, additional support to manage change, and an emotionally rich environment with the opportunity to build secure attachments with their key person, are especially vital for such children. In the next chapter, we will look at the role of the adult.

 Further information and references

Bombèr, L. (2020) *Know Me to Teach Me: Differentiated Discipline for Those Recovering from Adverse Childhood Experiences.* Broadway: Worth Publishing.

Brown, J. and Mather, M. (2014) *Foetal Alcohol Spectrum Disorder: Parenting a Child with an Invisible Disability.* Published by authors,

Brown, K. (2021) Domestic Abuse. Available at www.cps.gov.uk/domestic -abuse

Coram (2021) Fostering and adoption – Available at www.coram.org.uk

Coram BAAF (2021) Statistics: England – Looked After Children, Adoption and Fostering Statistics for England. Available at https://corambaaf.org.uk/ fostering-adoption/looked-after-children-adoption-fostering-statistics/stat istics-england

Department for Education (2018) Promoting the Education of Looked-After Children and Previously Looked-After Children: Statuary Guidance for Local Authorities. Available at https://assets.publishing.service.gov.uk /government/uploads/system/uploads/attachment_data/file/683556/Pr

omoting_the_education_of_looked-after_children_and_previously_loo
ked-after_children.pdf

FASD Network UK (2019) Available at www.fasdnetwork.org

Hughes, D. (2012) *Parenting a Child with … Emotional and Behavioural Difficulties*. London: British Association for Adoption and Fostering (BAAF).

Mental Health UK (2021) Available at 2021 https://mentalhealth-uk.org

Mind (2021) Available at www.mind.org.uk

National Organisation for FASD (2021) About FASD. Available at https://nationalfasd.org.uk/about-fasd/

NHS Surrey and Borders NHS Partnership Trust (2021) Foetal Alcohol Spectrum Disorders. Available at www.fasdclinic.com

NSPCC (2021) Parental Mental Health. Available at https://learning.nspcc.org.uk/children-and-families-at-risk/parental-mental-health-problems

Refuge (2017) Available at www.refuge.org.uk

Refuge (2020) 25% Increase in Calls to National Domestic Abuse Helpline Since Lockdown Measures Began. Available at www.refuge.org.uk/25-increase-in-calls-to-national-domestic-abuse-helpline-since-lockdown-measures-began/

Respect: Men's Advice Line (2019) Available at https://mensadviceline.org.uk

Roxby, P. (2020) Coronavirus: 'Profound' Mental Health Impact Prompts Calls for Urgent Research. Available at www.bbc.co.uk/news/health-52295894

SANE (2010–2021) Available at www.sane.org.uk

Social Care Institute for Excellence (2021) Domestic Violence and Abuse: Safeguarding During the COVID-19 Crisis. Available at www.scie.org.uk/care-providers/coronavirus-covid-19/safeguarding/domestic-violence-abuse

Sterne, A. and Poole, L. (2010) *Domestic Violence and Children: A Handbook for Schools and Early Years*. Abingdon: Routledge.

University of Bristol (2018) First UK Estimates of Children Who Could Have Conditions Caused by Drinking in Pregnancy Revealed. Available at http://bristol.ac.uk/news/2018/november/first-uk-prevalence-estimate-fasd.html

van der Kolk, B. (2014) *The Body Keeps the Score: Mind, Brain and Body in the Transformation of Trauma*. London: Penguin.

Women's Aid (2020) Available at www.womensaid.org.uk

Women's Aid (2021) What is Domestic Abuse? Available at www.womensaid.org.uk/information-support/what-is-domestic-abuse/

YoungMinds (2021) Available at https://youngminds.org.uk

4 | The role of the adult

In this chapter I am going to look at the role of the adult and how key this is for all children, but especially those with social, emotional and mental health needs.

The children I work with in Reception classes all have a teaching assistant, and on my first meeting with them I have three main messages about their role. Their job is to:

- love the child – for the child to arrive each day, and leave each day, knowing they are loved by this person
- create a safe space for the child
- help the child to co-regulate.

Professional love

For some staff the idea of loving a child leaves them feeling uneasy. I have had many conversations with staff, particularly teaching assistants, where they tell me it doesn't feel professional or they have safeguarding concerns about using the language of love in the context of children they work with. Within the Early Years, there is a growing amount of writing and research into the idea of professional love. Dr Jools Page (University of Sheffield n.d.) led a piece of research with 793 Early Years practitioners around the subject of professional love, aiming to understand the views of the Early Years sector on the place of love in the curriculum. She was aware, from her own direct work with children, that the relationship she built with the children she directly worked with was loving. The research results were very positive, with 95 per cent of the respondents having a positive attitude to the idea of professional love. Practitioners talked about how they felt comfortable with showing loving practices such as hugging and gentle touch to help build security and attachment. However, 10 per cent were worried about false accusations and other views about the appropriateness of their actions. Professionals were asked to describe professional love in their own words – terms used were 'care', 'kindness', 'paying attention'. As a follow-on from the research, Dr Page and her team produced an attachment toolkit and some videos as part of the Professional Love in Early Years Setting (PLEYS) project (University of Sheffield n.d.).

I took part in the original research group and I was really encouraged to read and hear about the findings. I do remember a time earlier on in my career when I heard Early Years staff telling me they were not to comfort physically or hug a child. It was encouraging to hear from Dr Page that this kind of thinking had mostly disappeared. Although the debate has re-emerged in light of Covid-19, at the point of writing this chapter nurseries and schools were having bubbles of the youngest children back into school in term six. The message throughout Covid-19 has been 'no hugging apart from the immediate household'. Many conversations have taken place across the country around how we respond to this when children return to our settings. My own personal view is that it is not realistic or appropriate to be trying to social distance with Early Years children, and if a child needs to be hugged or reassured then we need to be able to do this, while being aware of safety and hand washing. I know this has been hugely challenging for many people during this time, but I also know many Early Years professionals who have been able to make the return to their setting as normal as possible for children.

In schools, I think we sometimes see and hear different ideas around hugging and holding children. Safeguarding practice is extremely important, but if you have a child who approaches you and wants to be hugged, I feel it can be very damaging to turn them away. Many of the children we work with will need that gentle arm around their shoulder to reassure them, a gentle hand on their back to remind them they are not alone, a hug when they are distressed. For many of us, as adults, we know how that touch can feel comforting. It is just the same for children.

TAKE A MOMENT

Just for a moment, think about your feelings around professional love.

▶ How do you feel about the phrase 'professional love'?
▶ What are your feelings about appropriate and gentle touch with the children you care for?
▶ Have your views changed over the years?

Dr Page's initial research on the idea of professional love, this has been further developed and explored by Tamsin Grimmer (2021). In May 2020, Tamsin was interviewed by Kathy Brodie for Early Years TV, and talked about the subject of a loving pedagogy in the Early Years (see 'Further information and references'). She explores how children need to experience love in their early childhood setting, arguing that when children feel loved they are in a better place to learn. Tamsin encourages practitioners to have a loving pedagogy, recognising that love is a basic human need for all and that feeling loved is vital for children's wellbeing. She acknowledges that love is not just a feeling or an emotion, but a deliberate action – for example, acting in the best interests of someone else or enjoying spending time with others. She suggests we all love in many different ways and at different depths. For example, the love you feel for your mother is different from the one for your partner, and the affection you have for your own children is different from the one for the children you work with. Tamsin argues that a loving pedagogy is about putting children at the centre of our practice and she explores how this is not just confined to relationships. Some people question the difference between professional love and loving pedagogy. Tamsin suggests that the idea of professional love originally looked at the affectionate and caring behaviour of early childhood practitioners acting in place of parents and that this is needed to form healthy attachments. Tamsin has developed the notion to focus on how we need to develop a loving pedagogy by developing loving attachments, but also by embracing the loving pedagogy through everything we do: the environment we create, how we are with children in our interactions. So it's not just confined to the relationship, but it should underpin everything we do. For schools particularly, I think this is a really helpful addition to the conversation. A loving pedagogy is so important for all children, but for those with social emotional and mental health needs it is especially so, as they may not always have experienced that warmth and love from their caregivers. Later in the book, I will explore how we need to pay careful attention to the environment we provide, the support we offer and the messages we give to the children we work alongside.

An adult who is regulated

So far in this book, I have discussed how some children with social, emotional and mental health needs can communicate their strong, scared and frightened feelings in powerful, loud and sometimes violent ways. Some adults can interpret this as the child being naughty, intentionally difficult, out to get them. Sometimes adults can feel threatened or feel that they are being undermined by the child. I am not trying to belittle these very real feelings – when a child is hitting out, throwing or experiencing a complete emotional meltdown, this can be extremely hard to witness and manage, and can feel overwhelming. The key thing to remember is the child's behaviour is not about us or what we have done or whether or not they like us, but is frequently about them communicating how scared and unsafe they feel. As adults we are not always good at hearing that message; we can quickly jump to conclusions and make up a different story in our head. We need to learn to notice and listen to what the child is trying to tell us, and try to understand what is happening and what is going on for the child at that moment.

At all times, children need to feel safe, and part of them feeling safe is knowing that they can trust the adults around them, knowing that the adults are safe to be with. For some children, they do not have this experience at home, which is why it is even more important for them to experience this in their education and care setting. Children often know instinctively if the adult with them feels safe and can support them. By 'safety', I mean is not just physically protecting the child from hurting themselves, but also offering emotional safety. For example, if a child shouts at an adult in rage and goes to throw something at them and the adult responds by yelling at them, this does not feel safe. Children need adults who can regulate their own feelings and emotions. This is probably one of the most important roles of an adult. When a child feels dysregulated, they need an adult who can help them regulate, which we refer to as co-regulation – when the adult can soothe and support, can be empathetic and caring to the child while they are feeling distressed. Having a co-regulating adult with them will, over time, help the child to develop regulation strategies.

With early baby development, we know that a baby who is being held by a calm and gentle adult, whose heartbeat is steady, will also become calm. In contrast, when an adult picks up a baby, and they are stressed, their heart is beating quickly and their breathing is shallow, the baby will pick this up and become distressed themselves. It is the same with older children. When I arrive at a school or nursery, I can often tell within minutes how the children are going to be based on the adults. If they look agitated, distracted and stressed, the children will be more agitated and often more boisterous (staff often refer to them as being difficult). Children often mirror the adults in front of them. If you are in a situation and you find the children challenging, spend a moment to look at yourself and question how are you feeling. Are you stressed? The children are probably picking up these feelings from you.

When we start to feel stressed or threatened

When we work with children, it is so important that as key adults we are emotionally regulated and have an excellent emotional vocabulary and self-understanding. We need to be able to recognise when we are starting to feel stressed, anxious or agitated. Sadly, many of us have arrived at adulthood without having a very wide emotional understanding and vocabulary. I know many people who miss the warning signs their body is giving them to indicate they are stressed and becoming unwell.

There are many books on the subject of recognising stress and what it can do to your body, including *The Stress Solution* by Dr Rangan Chatterjee (2018). Brené Brown (2021) also talks about the need for emotional intelligence in her books. Her website lists 30 core emotion words that she thinks we should all know and also suggests that in practice most adults only know a handful of them. In 2019, Dr Marc Brackett, a professor at Yale University and director of the Yale Center for Emotional Intelligence, published *Permission to Feel*. On its inside front and back cover, he lists 100 emotion words. He challenges us to look at these and think about how we understand them and use them. I thought I had a good emotional vocabulary and understanding – I use both in my work all the time – but I was challenged by the 100 words. We can be very good at recognising when we are cross or happy or tired, but often this is where the emotion words stop.

I think we are not encouraged in the United Kingdom to recognise the emotions we feel. Irish theologian and poet Pádraig Ó Tuama (2016) uses the phrase 'Say hello to …' to recognise how you are feeling through the day. I found this particularly helpful at the beginning of the Covid-19 lockdown, when my feelings and emotions seemed to be like waves crashing over me. Some days they would quickly vary from anger, sadness, despair, apathy, but then sometimes optimistic and hopeful, to calm. I used his phrase a lot, to help me notice what was going on in my body and mind, and found it really helpful. I sometimes use it with the children I work with, and also use 'I wonder if you are feeling …' a lot. Other times, it can be helpful to something like: 'Lucy, let's say hello to the worry you feeling right now. It's OK to be worried.'

TAKE A MOMENT

Before we move on, take a minute or two to stop and consider how you know when you are stressed. What are the bodily warning signs? You may get headaches, your jaw might become tight or maybe you get irritable bowel syndorme. Our body tells us in many different ways when we are stressed, but often we ignore the signals or we are not aware that it is warning us.

Then think about your emotional vocabulary. How rich is it? Which words do you use to describe your emotions? Also, think about how aware you are of your varying emotions.

In Chapter 12, on the wellbeing of adults, I will look at stress in more detail and address some of the current thinking about how we deal with it.

Interview with Kieran McCarthy

Kieran McCarthy is the director of Brighter Futures, the organisation I work for. He used to be a Geography teacher and a headteacher of a residential school for children with SEMH needs, and is also a Thrive (2021) trainer.

 We know it is so important that adults are regulated and calm. Can you explain how this makes a difference to a child?

When a child has repeated experience of being soothed and calmed by adults who are themselves regulated, this supports the development of the child's stress regulation system at a physiological, emotional and cognitive level. In other words, the child learns how to regulate their body, their emotions and their thoughts through the experience of being regulated. Without that experience, children won't know how to cope with stress, as it won't be built into their nervous system. There is recent research on the physiological regulation between parents and children [see Suga et al. 2019]. The study measured the heart rhythms and breathing rate of mother and child. When the mother's heart rate and rhythms were regulated, then the child's heart rate was also steady and regulated.

Was this research with babies?

The research was done with children from 0 up until 4 or 5. What was interesting was the biggest synchronicity seemed to be with those children aged 6 months to a year. This provides further evidence that the Early Years are so important for the child's emotional development, and lays the foundation for a child's capacity for emotional regulation and resilience.

What about children who have not had a positive early development?

I see the positive impact for older children and teens when they have repeated, consistent experiences of being supported and regulated by the key adults in their life, even if they have missed out on this support in their Early Years. The capacity of the adults to regulate themselves is clearly connected with this.

What happens to the child if they are with someone who is stressed?

I am not a medical professional or scientist, but my understanding of the impact of stress on the body is like this.

If a child is around someone who is stressed, there is going to be a release of cortisol in their system as the child moves into survival mode. If this happens repeatedly, then the child's autonomic nervous system becomes wired for stress; their amygdala ('stress radar') becomes heightened or hypervigilant. The whole body is then reacting to even the smallest of sensory triggers or potential threats. The cortisol then stays in the body for hours. So, if the child is having repeated experiences of the adults around them being stressed, then the child's nervous system will be on high alert. This can be exhausting and overwhelming for the child, with their energy focused on 'survival'. It is very difficult to focus on learning, play or relaxed social interactions with peers if they do not feel safe with the adults around them. Contrasting with the child who is around a regulated adult, there may be stress happening, for the adult or child, but the adult can deal with the stress and help to make sense of the experience for the child; for example, 'I was in a rush and getting a little bit stressed, so I took some deep breaths and now I feel calm and ready to give you my full attention.' The child feels it at a physiological level – it's a moment of stress – but it passes. There might be a release of adrenaline for a moment, but adrenaline only lasts in the system for a few minutes. There isn't is a repeated release of cortisol in the brain and body, so the child is able to recover from the stress more quickly.

Sometimes our work can be stressful. How can staff help their stress levels?

From my experience of working in settings supporting children with SEMH needs, there needs to be a strong focus on staff wellbeing, supervision and support to identify, prevent and deal with stress. A whole school/setting approach, rather than leaving it to individual staff to manage stress on their own. Not surprisingly, I have seen children display more acting-out behaviours and greater level of distress during the times when staff stress levels are high, when staff feel less confident to deal with difficult situations, less empowered or unsupported – for example, when regular team meetings, opportunities for reflective practice or staff supervision is not in place. One level is preventive if we can have a daily wellbeing practice, and that will be different for everyone. For me it's time in nature, meditation and exercise.

To prevent stress, supporting staff wellbeing needs to be part of the ethos and culture of the school or setting, enabling and supporting all staff to prioritise their emotional health and wellbeing on a daily basis, and having support systems in place to monitor and address high levels of stress. I think it is also helpful to explore tools and strategies for dealing with stress as it inevitably arises. When something happens in the moment and we know our flight/fight/freeze response is triggered, the key is recognising this is a difficult moment and having a strategy. For me, this is taking five breaths and noticing what is happening in my body and mind. It's about self-awareness and staff being aware of their own emotional triggers. There is value in taking three or four deep breaths; it allows us to take a moment to pause, steady ourselves and reconnect our thinking brain.

When we are with a child who is in a state of emotional distress or anger, our amygdala may also be triggered into a survival reaction. In this stressful situation, we might struggle to respond to the child's needs in that moment. We might become reactive or shut off, whereas what the child needs is for us to be regulated, responsive and be able to think and act clearly. In these tricky moments we can regulate our breathing, calm our own stress system and think of strategies that we know can help, including turning to a colleague to ask for assistance if necessary. Working as a team is crucial for this.

The next question is, 'How do we develop self-awareness?' I think that is part of staff development for settings and schools. Thrive training and mindfulness training can help that. Also team culture can help – encouraging each other to give constructive feedback about what worked and helped, or what could be done differently. The importance of reflective practice is key.

In many ways what Kieran is describing is quite simple. These are not complicated strategies to use with children. They are strategies that can work for all of us in our families, with partners, with our parents, and with colleagues when they are having a moment of distress. However, they take practice and self-reflection. What I have learned most in this role, and from my colleagues such as Kieran, is that self-awareness is so important, but (as Kieran mentions) self-compassion is essential, too. There will be days when it all goes wrong, when we are having an off day. Being able to recognise this, learn from it, apologise to the child when we get it wrong, and being kind to ourselves, is so vital. Kristin Neff has been a huge help for me in my thinking and practice around this, as has her book *Self-Compassion* (Neff 2011).

A key part of working with children when that are dysregulated is to help them understand that we see them, we recognise what is going on for them and we are there to help keep them safe. This helps children to know they are not alone and that we are not judging them.

Staff supervision

We know that supporting children who have SEMH needs can sometimes be challenging. At times it can bring stresses and anxiety with the role, and sometimes it can feel very lonely. All the children we work with in schools have a teaching assistant to support them. I have worked with some of the most dedicated and committed teaching assistants, who show up every day, support the child, often act as their advocate, guide them, teach them, emotionally hold them and support them. A huge amount is expected from these staff. Sometimes they have teaching assistant training, sometimes they have specialist training on attachment and SEMH needs such as Thrive training, but often they don't. They are also often on low salaries and short-term contracts. It is not uncommon for a teaching assistant who is supporting a child with high SEMH needs to spend a lot of time outside the classroom, as the child finds time in the classroom too overwhelming. These staff can (and often do) feel easily forgotten. They must have regular supervision, where they have the opportunity to talk through what is happening, the strategies they are using, and to be given support. However, supervision is rare in many schools and often never happens. Within Early Years, there is now a requirement for staff to have supervision, but this is not the same in school – a situation that needs to change. Supervision offers staff support and guidance, and helps them to know they are not alone and not solely responsible for the child.

Along with supervision, other staff in the setting need to check in regularly with the key person/teaching assistant who is supporting the child, making sure they are OK and that the child is OK. In some situations, the days can be extremely challenging, with staff being hit, kicked or bitten. With some settings, I have noticed that this has become normalised and barely commented on. It is never OK for staff to be hurt – I am not saying that the children intend to hurt the adults, as I believe that in the majority of cases they do not – but we still need to acknowledge that, when a member of staff has been hit or bitten or had their hair pulled, this is a stressful experience. It is vital that other members of the team check in and make sure the adult is OK, give them some space to take some time out. I firmly believe that the adult has the time out, not the child. As colleagues, you could suggest they go and have a tea break or go for a walk around the block. Ask another member of staff to step in and support the child, and at the end of the day check in again that the staff member is OK and allow them to debrief from the day. The only way one-to-one staff can do their jobs well is when they have managers and a team supporting them, both emotionally and physically, through the words and actions they offer. Part of staff wellbeing in the team needs to be thinking about how the team supports one another. I will offer ideas around this in Chapter 12.

Conclusion

The children we work with are relying on us to support them. The most essential part of this is for us to help them with their regulation. We need to teach them skills and offer them tools to support with this. In the rest of the book, I will share ideas and tools that we can share with children.

 Further information and references

Brackett, M. (2019) *Permission to Feel*. New York: Macmillan.
Brown, B. (2021) List of Core Emotions. Available at https://brenebrown.com /downloads/
Chatterjee, R. (2018) *The Stress Solution: The 4 Steps to Reset Your Mind, Body, Relationships & Purpose*. London: Penguin.
Grimmer, T. (2020) Tamsin Grimmer on a Loving Pedagogy. Available at www.earlyyears.tv/episode/tamsin-grimmer-on-a-loving-pedagogy/
Grimmer, T. (2021) *Developing a Loving Pedagogy in the Early Years: How Love Fits with Professional Practice*. Abingdon: Routledge.
Neff, K. (2011) *Self Compassion*. London: HarperCollins.

Ó Tuama, P. (2016) *In the Shelter: Finding a Home in the World.* London: Hodder & Stoughton.

Suga, A., Uraguchi, M., Tange, A., Ishikawa, H. and Ohira, H. (2019) Research in Cardiac Interaction Between Mother and Child: Enhancement of Heart Rate Variability www.nature.com/articles/s41598-019-56204-5

Thrive (2021) The Thrive Approach. Available at www.thriveapproach.com

University of Sheffield (n.d.) Professional Love in Early Years Settings: A Report of the Summary of Findings. Available at https://pleysproject.files.wordpress.com/2017/06/pleys-report_singlepages.pdf

SECTION

II

5 | Environment

In Section I, I looked at some experiences that children with additional social, emotional and mental health (SEMH) needs may encounter. I also considered the role of the adult and how vital it is that adults be caring, supportive and regulated when working with children. Section II is going to explore some practical ways to support children, with ideas and suggestions for resources and activities for us to do and spaces we can create. All of these ideas are based on the daily work my colleagues and I carry out with the children we support. Sometimes it can feel overwhelming, and difficult to know what will help and support children who experience additional SEMH needs. I hope the practical ideas given in this section will prove helpful.

This chapter focuses on the environment. From my experience of working in schools and nurseries, I have observed that often the environment can be a trigger or place of agitation, or a difficult space for children with SEMH needs to be in. I wrote about Dan Siegel's (2020) idea of a window of tolerance in Chapter 1. Sometimes, when a child's window of tolerance is very narrow, the environment can become a trigger for them being outside of their window, and this causes overwhelming feelings or fear. When settings have a child who is not coping, I encourage staff to relook at the environment and try to see it through the eyes of a distressed child, and to be curious about what might be triggering them to feel unsafe or unsettled.

The environment as the third teacher

Some early years practitioners describe the environment as the third teacher, including those in Reggio Emilia, for whom it is a key part of their ethos. Reggio Emilia is a town in northern Italy and since the 1940s early years practitioners have been developing a unique way of educating pre-school children. Their method was originally started by a group of mothers who were unhappy with the education system, and it was then developed by educationist Loris Malaguzzi. The town developed its own 'Reggio approach' to education, which embeds creativity and the recognition that children express themselves through 'a hundred different languages'. It also believed that the environment has a vital role to play in educating and supporting the child (Edwards et al. 1998). If you visit the Reggio pre-schools, you will notice they pay huge attention to how the space looks and feels. I have been fortunate enough to take part in a study tour in Reggio. On my visit, one of the first observations I made was how uncluttered the spaces were, and also how light they were. These may sound like small additions, but they can have a huge impact on how a child responds in a space.

If you are unfamiliar with Reggio spaces, I would encourage you to stop reading for a moment and Google 'Reggio Emilia spaces' in 'Images', as this will show you what a wide range of the spaces look like. If the early years work in Reggio Emilia is new to you, see 'Further information and references'.

Natural resources

As well as uncluttered spaces, another key feature in Reggio pre-schools is the use of natural resources. You will often find wooden toys and equipment made from natural materials, but it is also common to see elements of the outside world brought to the inside environment – such as fresh flowers on the dining tables, sticks, feathers, pebbles, shells – which are used as part of loose parts play or as creative resources for children to use. Using natural resources is also a key element in Montessori practice and is also a common element in many Scandinavian settings. I have seen some fantastic examples of this in Denmark and Sweden. The main words I used to describe the spaces, when I first saw them, were 'beautiful', 'inviting' and 'calming'. They had created a space I wanted to stay in, an environment I wanted to explore and play in, but somewhere I felt I could sit in peacefully. I have to be honest, there are many times when those are the opposite feelings I have in some of the early years spaces I go into in the United Kingdom. I feel a little unfair writing that sentence, as I know many early years settings are working extremely hard to rethink their spaces. I know many settings that have managed to purchase beautiful wooden equipment and playthings – and there are spaces I go into in the United Kingdom which bring about similar feelings to those I experienced in Reggio and Scandinavia. However, you may have beautiful wooden objects and playthings, but it can still look and feel cluttered and overwhelming. So it's not just about the resources, but more about the underpinning ethos.

How the environment can be a sensory overload

We are all very sensitive to the environments we spend time in and it's no surprise that during the Covid-19 lockdown many people started to redecorate, declutter, even think about moving house. When we are in one environment all the time, it can have a great impact on our emotional and mental wellbeing. Of course, we all have different tastes and preferences: some people love the stripped-back minimalist approach, while others embrace cosiness and comforting things around them. For many people, especially if they have sensory or processing difficulties (which many children with SEMH challenges do), then clutter and too many things in an environment can be distressing.

I am now going to look at a few areas that can cause difficulties in the environment for some children.

Busy walls and displays

Some classrooms and nursery spaces have an amazing range of things on display, from pictures children have made, beautiful artistic colourful displays, notices and messages for parents, words in bold. I always find this interesting, and often wonder who the displays are for. A few questions I would ask are:

▶ Are the displays for the children?
▶ Are the displays for the parents?
▶ Are the displays for the manager?
▶ Are the displays for visiting advisors and inspectors?

Once you have established this, then break the answer down. If the display is for parents:

▶ Do they look at it?
▶ What messages are you trying to put over?
▶ Is it clear and easy to read?

If the display is for children:

▶ Can they see it?
▶ Do they understand why it is there?

▶ Do they look at it and engage with it?
▶ Were they involved in putting it together?
▶ How busy is the display?
▶ How colourful is the display?

The reason for asking these questions is that I think we often believe parents and children love displays, but in my experience they rarely look at and engage with them. Children's displays, for example, are regularly at a height where the child cannot see it well: if you can see the display, or have to look up to do so, then the children cannot see it properly, instead seeing lots of colour and stuff.

Some children have sensory difficulties, including visual processing ones (Abraham et al. 2015). When a child has visual processing difficulties, they might find the visual stimulation around them too distracting, or even distressing. Displays can be tricky for some children, as they can be visual clutter to them. Even if the display is not at child height, it can still be too much visually: the mix of colours, and maybe things hanging down, can cause overstimulation, which can be distressing for some children.

Hanging objects

▶ What hanging objects do you have in your space?
▶ Are there washing lines with children's paintings or creative work hanging down?
▶ Are there large mobiles hanging from the ceiling?
▶ Are there flags, banners or drapes?

Hanging objects are not always a sensory overload, but if there are a lot of them they can be visually noisy, especially alongside busy displays. Some settings use drapes and material effectively to create calming spaces, but, again, other types of hanging objects can cause visual overload.

Colour scheme and lighting

▶ What is the colour scheme in your space?
▶ Is it loud and colourful?
▶ Is it calming and subdued?
▶ How is the lighting? Do you have much natural light coming in?

▶ Do you have strip lighting?

▶ Do you have areas with dimmed lighting?

Many children will not notice the displays, colours and lighting. However, for some children, these things can be the difference between them feeling calm or feeling heightened and distressed.

We are beginning to understand how colours can impact our sense of calm or alertness, and thankfully lots of classrooms and nurseries are now painted in calmer colours rather than the bright colours that were used 10 or so years ago.

Children who have had a difficult start to the day can arrive, walk into a classroom or nursery room, notice the washing line of pictures hanging down or the flickering strip light, and this can cause them to fly into a rage. I have seen a child notice this and then run to hide.

For those children who don't seem to notice, having many colourful displays makes little difference, but it can be extremely distressing for those children with sensory difficulties. I am not suggesting you get rid of all the displays and hanging objects, but I do suggest you look very carefully at your visual environment.

TAKE A MOMENT

This is an activity you can do with your colleagues. If I am delivering training from their nursery, I often get staff to do this in training sessions.

Get everyone to kneel down or lie on their back. Look around the space. Ask them what they see from this height. What does it feel like?

This is a very simple exercise, but it helps us to see things from a child's height and/or view, and that it can look very different from how we usually see the environment.

As a follow-on exercise you could do with the children, ask them to photograph from their height the walls, displays and hanging things, discuss with them. What do they see? What do they like? What don't they like? This is a simple child's voice exercise you can perform, giving you a sense of how the children experience the space.

Children's involvement in creating the environment

Instead of staff creating the environment for the children, they could work together with the children on this. Involve children in thinking about the displays, what goes on them and what you have around the classroom. Have conversations with them about the colours you choose, the objects you select and encourage them to think about the resources you need and where you keep them. This gives children a greater sense of this being a shared environment – one that they all need to take care of, but also one that needs to meet everyone's needs.

I have worked in a setting where they totally changed the environment for a few weeks. One nursery where I worked were involved in a project that was thinking about how to bring the outside inside, and one child wondered what would happen if the outside was inside. Over one weekend, the staff put turf into the nursery – the whole of the floor was covered in grass turf. Everything else was taken outside and the children arrived to a room of grass. It stayed for a few weeks, and the children and staff together enjoyed playing and planning how to use a room of grass. This is a slightly mad example! But I love it as an example of listening to children's thoughts and thinking differently.

Clutter

'Clutter' means that there are lots of things around. Some people can live with it and not notice, yet for others it can be a huge irritant. Personally, I fall somewhere in the middle, as I can live with some clutter, but when I am stressed I am more sensitive to it. I know that for some settings – the nursery room, classrooms or the space available for childminding – there may be limited physical and storage space. This is especially an issue in school classrooms, I've noticed. When we have limited room and lack of storage space, clutter can sometimes be more of a problem, and also, as the years progress, it can grow. In some school classrooms, this can look like lots of tables and chairs, boxes with things inside, an overflowing junk modelling area, loads of boxes of toys and resources, a dressing-up area with overflowing clothes in a box or on a rail.

There are a few problems with having lots of clutter:

▶ It can be hard for children to find the tools and toys they want.
▶ It can be visually overwhelming.
▶ For some children, it can feel unsafe.

Ideally, we want children to see or know what toys and resources are available to them. Of course, this doesn't mean having everything out on show, but for children to know what is available for them to access. The difficulty with having lots of clutter is the same as having too much visual stimulation: some children can find this overwhelming. It can also cause difficulties in accessing or finding what they require, which can lead to frustration and sometimes dysregulation. Some children find that clutter brings about unsafe feelings for them. They don't know what is there or not there, and it can sometimes lead to children feeling anxious.

The other difficulty with lots of clutter is that children can find it hard to move freely around the space. I have seen spaces where there is so much covering the floor area – even before children get out the toys, games, etc. – that they are falling over and stepping on things. It can feel like an obstacle course to get around the space. Once again, this can feel overwhelming and unsafe for some children (and adults, too!).

TAKE A MOMENT

This is an exercise that can be good to do as part of a team meeting. As a team, spend time looking around your nursery/classroom.

- ► What do you notice?
- ► Does everything in your room have a home/a space where it lives?
- ► Do children know how to find things?
- ► Do you need everything that is out on display?
- ► When was the last time you had a sort-out?

Often settings will have a big sort-out around once a year. This is an opportunity to sort through resources, get rid of things that are not needed – a bit like a spring clean. But, it might be worth doing this more often, maybe every few months. I am not suggesting throwing away resources, but it can be good practice to relook, declutter regularly, maybe put some things away in storage (if you have some storage space available to you). You could involve the children in this, getting them to think about the resources they use and love and those they never play with.

Quiet spaces

Many of the children I work with frequently become overwhelmed in the noisy spaces in a classroom or nursery room. Whenever I enter a new nursery room or classroom, where I am going to be supporting a child, I always look for a quiet space. This might be a book corner or an area with drapes and cushions and blankets; or it might be a tented area, or even a den under a table. For me, every setting needs to have a quiet space, a place where children can sit, lie down and find some peace. I would also advocate for these spaces to be available outside as well as inside.

When we have quiet spaces, we need to make sure all the children in the setting know what this area is for and understand how to use it. Children won't just know this, though. We need to tell them, show them, model to them how to use this space. It is also important that children can access this when they need to. Some children will never enter this space, but for others it will be their place of safety and solace. It's important that these spaces are gender-neutral. I often see quiet spaces that look and feel very feminine, with pink curtains and fluffy cushions. Some boys will love this, but other boys (and girls) will hate it and find it very off-putting. it is important to give some thought to the colours and type of material you use.

Elizabeth Jarman has been researching and working on the idea of communication-friendly spaces, which has been an area of her work for many years. She suggests that many busy, cluttered classrooms and early years spaces do not encourage children's communication. They can often also be noisy, which again inhibits good communication. For children to be able to communicate well with each other and with adults, she proposes they need spaces that are inviting and accessible for communication.

Elizabeth advocates using calming colours on the walls, drapes and soft lighting, and having areas where there are cushions, blankets, rugs – comfortable places to sit or lie. She encourages using natural objects or items that have been upcycled from our homes. When I have been in early years settings influenced by Elizabeth's ideas, I have noticed how much calmer they feel, and also how calm the children are. What I like about Elizabeth's work is that she does not advocate huge financial outlay on expensive wooden, specially made equipment and toys. She welcomes, and encourages, staff and families to use things from the home and adapt them for the setting. See the links to Elizabeth's work in 'Further information and references'.

Hygge

Early years settings that have used Elizabeth's ideas remind me of a Danish nursery I visited, where the idea of hygge is an important part of the culture (Hygge in the Early Years 2021). This is about creating a safe, cosy feel in their setting. In the nursery I visited, the main furniture in the room was comfy sofas and cushions, along with sheepskin rugs on the floor. The lighting was soft, from lamps and fairy lights. They had house plants and items they had found in the surrounding woodland (such as feathers, seedpods and some bones), which were displayed in a glass cabinet as objects of beauty and wonder. The setting also had stuffed animals around the space – I must admit I haven't yet encountered that in a nursery in the United Kingdom – but it provided a sense of awe and wonder. What I observed in this Danish nursery, and through talking to the staff, was that the children and staff were incredibly calm and peaceful. A huge amount of their time was spent outside and in the woods, and this certainly played a big part in supporting the children's wellbeing and sense of calm. (I look at this more in Chapter 9, 'Outdoors'). However, I also believe the feel of the indoor space also helped the children and staff to feel calmer. It was a place that felt inviting and comfortable, safe and homely, and encouraged you to snuggle in and relax. In the United Kingdom, Kimberly Smith has a consultancy and training service that supports early years settings in implementing and practising hygge. This is a mix of looking at the resources you provide, the environment you create and also ideas for outdoor and indoor provision. A link to this is at the end of the chapter.

TAKE A MOMENT

▶ Do you have quiet spaces in your setting, both inside and outside?
▶ How well are these used by the children? You may want to spend a few days observing how the children use the space.
▶ What do the children think about the space? You could ask the children to take photos or tell you how they like to use the space and what they like about it. If you have children who never use the space, find out what they think, too.

Specific calming areas

It is not unusual for the children we work with to become overwhelmed and dysregulated. Sometimes the environment contributes to that (as discussed above); other times it can be because a request has been made or a transition is happening; and other times we have no idea what has upset the child. As mentioned in Chapter 4, in the interview with Kieran McCarthy, ideally adults can recognise when a child is beginning to struggle and get in there to offer support and diffuse the situation before it erupts, but that is not always possible. One tool we regu-larly use, and recommend to settings, is a safe and calming space for the child to use. We often use a tepee or pop-up tent for this, but I have also used a large cardboard box or made an improvised tented space under a table with a blanket covering the table.

The purpose of this space is that the child can go in there when they need a space that feels safe and calming. This is not a time-out space – we do not use time out, always time *in*, with a child. This space is about it being safe and secure, and we often put a few soft items in there. The box below provides a list of pos-sible items to go in the area. It will often be slightly darker than the rest of the classroom, as this lower light can help the child feel calmer. Ideally, the calming area would still be in the classroom/nursery room – not away in a corridor, but still part of the class/group. Having it in the main room enables the child to have some time to gently calm down and reach a place of regulation, without feeling that they are being sent away as a punishment. The other point of the calming area is that the adults are alongside the child: if not physically in the space with them (it's not always possible for an adult to fit in), they are just outside.

If you have a child in your class or group with recognised additional SEMH needs or other sensory issues, ideally you will have a specific calming area for that child. For example, at the end of Term 6 last year, I discussed with three of my new schools how we were going to put this in place for the child I would be supporting in September. We had heard from their nurseries that a tented space worked, so wanted to make sure this was in place at the beginning of the autumn term. The whole class was told it was that particular child's area and not a general play space. Some settings are worried that the other children in the class won't accept this or that it won't be fair on them. In my experience, children are far more accepting than we give them credit for, and rarely protest or insist on using it.

What to have in a quiet space

As mentioned above, the quiet space could be:

▶ a pop-up tent
▶ a tepee
▶ a table with blankets covering it, so the child can go underneath
▶ a clothes horse with blankets covering it

▶ a very large cardboard box with a blanket covering it (perhaps get the child to decorate it).

Imagine a den space that you may have made as a child or with your own children. The attraction of these spaces is that they are small, dark and cosy. Make it cosy inside, with blankets, cushions and fairy lights (or small LED candles).

Some children like to have a favourite toy or a few books in the space, while others prefer to have some fiddle toys or a calming box (see Chapter 8 for more ideas on this). It's important that children are involved in making it just for them.

How to use these spaces

When they are being calm, tell the child about the calming area you have created. Explain that this is going to be their space, where they can spend some time with you, and that it is a place that can help them to feel a bit calmer. Involve the child in thinking about what they would like in it. Maybe they can choose the blankets and material from ones you have available, and select the cushions they would like in there. One child I worked with did not want cushions. He wanted one very thin blanket and his favourite toy. I have also worked with a child who wanted five blankets, and he would totally cover himself in these. As we know, every child is different, and they will know what feels good to them and what does not. We want this space to feel good for them.

This space is never to be used as a punishment. I do not believe in time out with children – what they need is time in with a calm and caring adult. This space is about enabling the child to have some time away from the things that are overwhelming them. This is a space that is intended to feel safe, a place where they can connect with an adult.

How to use a calming space

Explain that you will be with them and it is to help them feel safe. When you can see the child is beginning to fizz and become dysregulated, you need to say to the child, 'I can see you are beginning to feel a bit cross. Let's go and sit in your quiet space. I think it might help you to feel a bit calmer.' By using these words, you are showing the child that you have recognised the strong feelings they have, and you are validating these and helping to contain the child. It takes time and practice, and it won't always work, but by being calm and consistent these spaces can be so helpful.

Over time you hope to get to a place where the child recognises and chooses to take themselves into the quiet space. Last year I supported a boy who could become extremely violent very quickly. At first, we found it extremely hard to know what the triggers were or to anticipate them, and we used a calming space and calming box with him, consistently. Sometimes it was the teaching assistant with him; other times the teacher; and sometimes members from the senior leadership team (headteacher included). They would sit and be with him in the space, helping him to find some calmness. Partway through the year, he started to say to staff, 'I am feeling cross. I just want to sit in my space.' This felt like a positive breakthrough. Of course, there were still times when he wasn't able to recognise the rising feelings, but it showed us that this space became a place he acknowledged as being safe, and importantly he was beginning to learn and see in himself the variety of feelings and emotions. (I will look at this more in Chapter 7, on emotional language and recognising feeling and emotions.)

A sensory break

Some of the children I work with find group time/carpet time extremely difficult. The process of sitting can be tricky, as there may be lots of sensory distractions with other children around them. Some of these children have found that being in their quiet space at the back of the classroom during carpet time feels OK. From there, they can hear and see (if they choose to, by poking their head out) what is happening, and that can feel safer. It can be the sensory break they need. I had one little boy who for months did all the class phonics time from his tented space with his teaching assistant. He didn't fall behind; this space worked for him. Eventually, he was able to move out of the tent and be part of the rest of the class, but on other days, when he was struggling, he was able to go back to using the tented area.

Conclusion

The environment is not always the first thing we think about when we are supporting children with SEMH needs. Instead, often our default is to think about behaviour. However, if we take a step back and think curiously about the environment we have created – if we relook at it through the eyes of a child, and wonder how they may feel about the space and what their experience may be – this could help us to find some solutions and assist us in the holistic approach to working with children and finding ways to aid and support them. Sometimes it is just small changes and tweaks that we need to make, but these small changes can be enough to make a big difference to a child.

If thinking about the environment is a new idea for you, I would encourage you to take some time as a team and think about the specific needs of your current cohort of children and then look at how the inside and outside environment assists, or may exasperate, these needs. This will benefit all your children and staff. For me, this is something we need to do regularly – certainly with each new cohort of children, as every group of children will have different sensory needs.

📖 Further information and references

Abraham, D., Heffron, C., Braley, P. and Drobnjak, L. (2015) *Sensory Processing 101*. LLA Media LLC.

Edwards, C., Gandini, L. and Forman, G. (eds) (1998) *The Hundred Languages of Children: The Reggio Emilia Approach – Advanced Reflections*. London: Ablex Publishing.

Hygge in the Early Years (2021) Hygge in the Early Years. Available at www.hyggeintheearlyyears.co.uk

Jarman, E. (2021) Elizabeth Jarman: Creating Optimum Conditions for Learning. Available at https://elizabethjarman.com

Reggio Emilia Approach (2020) Reggio Emilia Approach. Available at www.reggiochildren.it/en/reggio-emilia-approach/

Siegel, D. (2020) *The Developing Mind: How Relationships and the Brain Interact to Shape Who We Are*, 3rd edition. New York and London: Guilford Press.

Smith, K. (2021) How You Can Harness 'Hygge' in Early Years. Available at www.teachearlyyears.com/learning-and-development/view/how-you-can-harness-hygge-in-early-years

6 | Routines and transitions

This chapter explores how routines and transitions are vital for all children, but especially children who have additional social, emotional and mental health (SEMH) needs. Transitions and preparing for transitions have become a key part of my world, and once you start working in this way it soon permeates to other parts of your life. To my family's amusement (and sometimes irritation) I spend lots of time making sure we are all prepared for the different transitions – I don't think you can overprepare.

In the run-up to a child starting school or nursery, we are often good at thinking about the transition, the support we can offer, the information we need to share and the different ways we can prepare. However, we don't always think about some of the transitions that happen at other times, particularly the small ones. In this chapter, I will explore some of these smaller transitions, and the practices we can put in place to support them. Many books have been written about supporting children in the bigger transitions, and I list a couple of these in 'Further information and references' (Grimmer, 2018; Mainstone-Cotton, 2020). For some children, all transitions, particularly small ones, can lead to high anxiety and cause them to go into fight/ flight/freeze mode.

TAKE A MOMENT

Before we continue, spend a moment thinking about how many transitions the children you work with go through in a day.

You might want to start with the children's transitions before they arrive at nursery or school Here are some examples:

▶ getting up
▶ having breakfast

► getting washed
► getting dressed
► leaving the house.

Then, once they arrive, maybe break your day up into:

► arrival
► morning routine
► lunch
► afternoon routine
► leaving.

When I have done this exercise, it has made me realise how many transitions the children I support encounter in a day. The next question to ask is: 'Are they expecting these transitions?" Do they know what to expect? Do they need to do all these transitions?

Power

For some children, change and transitions are no problem. Some children appear to be adaptable – they can roll with whatever is taking place and accept it all – but, in my experience, many do find change and transitions tricky. I think most children want to understand what is happening, and to know about the change that is about to take place. It's the same for us as adults. How happy are you when something suddenly changes? For example, imagine you are sitting reading a book and your partner comes into the room and announces, 'Put your coat on – we are going out.' Would your response be 'OK', and you follow the instruction without question? I know I would respond by asking, 'Why – where are we going? Why now?' and I would probably feel quite irritated and annoyed (maybe very cross that I hadn't been told about it before), and I may refuse. Often it comes down to power. As adults, we have all the power, and usually we make the decisions about what we do, when and how. Some adults are great at involving children in these when it is appropriate, but often we hold the power and we don't always think about its impact.

For me, part of the problem is that we just don't think enough about the changes. We don't think in terms of lots of small transitions and changes – we just do it. I hope this chapter will help us to reflect on these small adjustments a little more.

Why transitions can be challenging

In Section I, we looked at a variety of experiences encountered by some children with SEMH needs. If a child's early life has been confusing, frightening and overwhelming, or if the child processes the world differently and they experience many things as overwhelming and frightening, then they often want to have some control over things, control over their small world. Many of the children we work with are described as needing to be in control the whole time. I am often told by staff and parents that a child is fine if they are doing what they want, but, as soon any demand is put on them, they will explode. This explosion, and anger, is usually coming from a place of fear, maybe a place of confusion. The child is often not able to articulate how they are feeling, but the experience has triggered a fight/flight (or sometimes freeze) response. For some children, it is not anger they respond with, but to freeze. I worked with one girl a few years ago, who – when she was told it was time to go to lunch or go outside to play, or to line up for assembly – would lie down wherever she was, close her eyes and just stay. She didn't fight or kick or make a noise. No amount of coaxing, or trying to persuade her to move, would work. She froze. The adults working with her found this infuriating and the lens they were viewing it through and the story they told themselves was that she was intentionally being stubborn and difficult. I tried to help them see this through the lens of a girl who was being overwhelmed by the change. She needed preparation and support, not being told off.

How does it feel?

As I mentioned above, for some children these changes can feel frightening, overwhelming and confusing. We know why we have asked the child to do the next change, but do they? It is recognised as good practice to prepare all children for changes or transitions, and that all children benefit from this. However, sometimes we can forget that some children need preparation for each small transition or change, particularly if it is one they have not chosen.

Below are some case studies based on practice I have observed over the years, along with some suggestions as to how it could look different. (Names have been changed for confidentiality.)

CASE EXAMPLES

Assad is 6 months old. He is lying on the floor under a baby gym, laughing, watching and gurgling. His parent comes over, picks him up, and suddenly puts his coat on to go outside. The parent does not speak to Assad, who may be wondering what has happened, and feel cross, or surprised, maybe frightened. An alternative approach could be for the parent to kneel and watch Assad for a moment, stroke his cheek, have eye contact with him and tell him, 'You are enjoying this, but we need to put your coat on and go out to the shops.' Assad is not going to understand the words, but the process is slower, there is a connection made and it feels safer. Assad may still complain and grumble or maybe cry, but the parent will hopefully soothe and reassure, recognising that he is protesting at the change.

Favour is 2 years old. He is playing in the sandpit when a nursery worker comes over and announces that it is lunchtime. The worker lifts Favour, takes him to the sink to wash his hands, and then puts him into a highchair. Favour responds by screaming and kicking. As they approach the sink, he starts to flail his hands even more, and by the time they get to the highchair Favour has totally lost it – his arms and legs are all over the place. Favour is highly agitated and the worker is struggling to hold him. Favour may be feeling shocked, anger and rage, and maybe worry. An alternative approach would be for the worker to come over to Favour, kneel next to him, engage with Favour in the sand, then show him a sand timer and explain, 'When the sand has gone through, we are going to wash our hands and it will be lunchtime. After washing hands, I will put you in the highchair.' The worker may also have some small visual images to show Favour, too.

Maddie, aged 3 years, has arrived at the nursery and goes straight over to the Duplo area. She works intently on a construction. Other children come over and join her and then move on. Maddie stays here for 30 minutes – she knows what she is building and continues to adjust and alter her construction. A member of staff shakes a rainstick and announces, 'It is snack time. Everyone needs to stop and tidy away what they are doing. After snack, it will be singing time.' Maddie appears to ignore this and continues to build. Staff notice that Maddie is the only child not tidying up and call across the room to remind her. Maddie ignores them and continues with her construction. All the other children have tidied up and are now sitting down for a snack. Maddie continues to build, seemingly unaware of what is happening around her. A member of staff comes over to Maddie and tells her again she has to tidy away. Maddie ignores her, the staff member starts to pack away the Duplo, Maddie suddenly screams and continues to scream, and the member of staff is unable to calm Maddie. Maddie may be feeling shocked and furious. An alternative approach would be for Maddie's keyworker to approach Maddie while she was playing, notice what she was doing and how hard she was working on it, engage with Maddie, and talk about what she was making. At this point, they could use a personalised 'Now and Next' tool (see below), showing Maddie a picture of Duplo 'Now' and snack 'Next'. Five minutes before the rainstick, the keyworker could go back to Maddie, notice the progress she has made and warn her, 'In five minutes, the rainstick will be shaken for tidy-up time, and then it will be snack time.' They could show her a picture of tidy-up time on the visual prompts on their key fob and the 'Now and Next'. When the rainstick is shaken, the keyworker could go over to Maddie, explain that they know she has worked so hard. The two of them could decide where her construction can be stored for safety, then put the remaining Duplo away together.

TAKE A MOMENT

Take a moment to think about how you prepare children in your setting for transitions. Do you always prewarn them? Do all your staff use the same techniques? Preparing children for small transitions can easily be overlooked. It is one of those topics worth exploring and reflecting on as a team.

Routines

I am including the idea of routines in this chapter as routine can be beneficial for children, especially young children. Many adults also find routines helpful.

TAKE A MOMENT

For a moment, think through your day. Do you have regular routines in your day that support you? Think about those routines and consider how they help you get through the day. It may be having a coffee in the morning or exercising. Or it may be the routine at the end of the day which helps you to switch off.

I have a morning routine from Monday to Friday. I get up around 5.45 a.m., have a drink of water, drive to my local pool for my morning swim, swim for 30 minutes, come back, have a coffee and then check emails. For many people, one of the initial problems with the Covid-19 lockdowns was the loss of their regular routine. I swapped my swim with a sunrise walk, as I knew I needed to keep the habit of a routine going, and I think that hugely benefited my mental health during lockdown. In the way that many of us have learned how important it is to have some form of routine, it is the same for children. I am not suggesting we need rigid routines – for example, stopping every 40 minutes to change an activity. However, a general routine, which all the children know and learn, can help them to feel safe and secure. This may include a routine around welcoming time, lunchtime and end of the day.

For some of the children we work with, their lives at home can sometimes be chaotic, and for others their home lives can be filled with many changes. Children can cope with change, especially if the adults around them are calm and coping, but they also cope better when they are prepared and when they know what is happening. There are some very simple ways we can achieve that in the setting, and we can also encourage parents to use these tools at home. In the next part of this chapter, I am going to look at some of the tools we can use to support children in preparing them for the routine and any changes.

Tools to support

Waiting time

Sometimes a child becomes overwhelmed because we have given them too much information. I know I can be guilty of doing that. I may give two or three instructions at once, but all the child can hear is the first part, which is sometimes their name. Then they are prone to switch off, or sometimes they become distressed at feeling overwhelmed at the instructions. This situation is easily lessened by breaking it down, slowing down what we are asking and separating it into segments. For example, 'Summer.' Then wait while you get her attention: 'It's time to get your coat.' Then, when the coat is on: 'We are going outside now.' Kerry Payne (2020) describes this as the 'waiting time' (see 'Further information and references'). For some children the verbal slowing down is enough, whereas other children may need an object of reference, which could be a picture or pointing to an object – in this example, the coat. Waiting time can also be the length of time we expect a child to wait. This can become a problem, and one I often see in schools, especially where you are waiting for one or two children to do something. For example, maybe you ring your bells and all children are expected to stand still and wiggle their fingers. Most of the class do this, but one or two struggle, so you wait and you tell the child, 'We are all waiting for you.' I have seen examples of a teacher waiting 10 minutes before finally the whole class did what was asked. In my opinion, this waiting is not really benefiting anyone, and it is certainly leading the teacher to feel stressed. Maybe the children you know are going to find this difficult could be given some assistance? Maybe one of them could ring the bells, and another could be given a different job. I do understand, when there is a class of 30 children and only two adults,that it is not always possible to individually support the children who need it, but there may be some other creative ways we can rethink some of these tricky moments.

Visual timetables

A lot of early years settings and Reception classes use visual timetables, but sadly the practice is not common beyond Reception age. The visual timetable is an excellent tool to show children what will happen during the day, breaking it down into visual prompts – for instance, hand washing, arrival, lunch, going home. Many settings have one for all the children, often at a key place in the room, to be used at the start of the day to remind the children of the plan for the day. When staff know individual children need additional support, it is a good idea for them to have a few of the cards on a lanyard, which they can use to show and remind the child what is happening next. You can buy them, but many practitioners make their own, as it is so easy. (Ideas for sourcing images are listed in 'Further information and references'.)

'Now and Next' boards

The visual timetable is useful, but some children may struggle to retain all the information and need the immediate – that is, 'Now' and 'Next' prompts. These boards are incredibly simple, often a homemade laminated sheet with two boxes: one labelled 'Now', the other 'Next'. They have Velcro on each box and a range of pictures representing all the different daily activities, and the idea is you find the relevant image to go on the boxes and stick these on with the Velcro. The keyworker will use this to show the child what is happening 'Now' and then 'Next'. Alternatively, staff may have a whiteboard and draw on a 'Now' and 'Next' symbol.

Many of the children I support have 'Now and Next' boards. Sometimes they are only needed at the start of the year, and then, as the child settles into the routine they need it less, but other children need it throughout the year (I encourage staff to send it through to the Year 1 class). Children often enjoy taking ownership of this and finding the relevant images and sticking them on the box. It's important to have a wide range of images to capture the different parts of the day. For the children I support, nurture time is a key part of their day and the staff will have an image for this. They also use a photo of me to show them the sessions when I am in school to come and work with them. One of the children I supported last year had his own 'Now and Next' and visual timetable, and at the start of the lockdown the school made a similar resource for Mum to use at home, which she used to help her structure his day. She also made some new cards to fit with family life, and found it a helpful tool during a tricky time.

With the visual timetable and 'Now and Next' cards, it is a good idea to use the same package/images throughout, and (if possible) to share these with parents for them to use at home. You can use many different types of images – for example, PECS, Makaton, real photos. Kerry Payne advocates (2020) making sure that whatever you use is consistent, as it can become very confusing for children if we use a wide variety of images.

Task cards

Along with the tools mentioned above, some children also find it useful to have images for the sequencing of some tasks, such as washing hands. If you have the visual prompt and reminder in a place where the child can see, this can assist and support all the children, especially those who find following instructions hard.

Pictures of staff/parents

Many of the children I work with need to know which adults are supporting them, or are going to be in the setting. They can find staff changes unsettling. Many early years settings use a photo board at the entrance that shows who is in the nursery that day. Individual classes in schools also do this sometimes. In one school I worked with, there were job-share teachers and job-share teaching assistants, and at the start of the school year we made a visual booklet. The child had this at home, with a day on each page, and each page would show (with photos) which staff members were supporting them that day. This visual resource helped the parents to support the child each morning before they arrived at school, and it became part of the routine to look at the booklet to help the child as they prepared for the day.

This idea can also be used to support children when they leave the setting if the child is regularly picked up by different people during the week – for example, different parents or childminders, or other family members. This is a helpful tool to use if the child finds the transition of leaving difficult. Using pictures of the person who is collecting is a useful tool. You might use this on a 'Now and Next' board, as part of the visual timetable or have a staff booklet (as described above). One boy I worked with had four different people collecting him each week, which he found confusing and distressing. We had photos of each person, and at lunchtime we would show him which person was collecting him that day. We would then remind him again partway through the afternoon. His mum used the same technique and would show him the photo in the morning, explaining whose day it was to pick him up. We have also used something similar for a child who was co-parented and lived in Mum's house one part of the week and Dad's house the other. In the afternoon, the staff used a photo of the parent and the house the child was going to at the end of the day, which helped prepare and remind them.

Stories/social stories when bigger change happens

We use social stories a lot in our work. They help children understand a change or transition or if they need help with a particular issue, such as toileting or mealtimes. You can buy social stories, but they are easy to write yourself, and that way you can address the exact issue you need to be covered.

One example of a social story we use is around transitioning to school. The story has photos of a girl called Lily, who is about to start school. It talks through what will happen and addresses her feelings about this. It also asks some questions, such as:

▶ Lily is going to her new school. It is called Camerton Primary. Where are you going to school?
▶ Lily's school jumper is blue. What colour will your school jumper be?
▶ Lily is going to school with her friend Megan. Which friends are going to your new school?
▶ Lily will be going to school on the bike with her dad. How will you get to school?
▶ Lily will be having school lunches at school – she likes eating jacket potato. What will you do at lunchtime?
▶ Lily is looking forward to playing with the pirate boat in the classroom. What are you looking forward to at school?
▶ Lily is a little bit worried about playtimes – the playground has a big climbing frame and she is a bit scared about that. Does anything worry you about school?

This is a simple tool, with a photo and a paragraph on each page. Using something like this helps you to support, remind and prepare the child, but also allows you to hear their thoughts or concerns.

Knowing what is going to happen

As I mentioned at the beginning of the chapter, for some children the not knowing can be distressing, and when they are distressed they can show this by shouting or hiding or refusing. If we can let children know what is due to happen that day, that can lower their anxieties.

I have just finished working on a two-week playscheme during the summer holidays, which was aimed at primary-aged children who have found lockdown especially challenging. Some of the children who attended struggled with anxious feelings, and for some children not knowing what was going to happen made this worse. Our playscheme was about offering high-quality art, sport, play and outdoor experiences, underpinned with a high nurture ethos.

We put in place a very simple structure to support the children. Each morning they were welcomed by the same members of staff, and were walked on to the site by a member of staff who was smiling, caring and checking in with them. We started each session with everyone sitting around the firepit, where the adults told the children about the different resources. The aim was for the adults to provide resources and ideas, but also to follow the children's lead and interests, so these were not set activities but loose ideas. We followed the same structure each day and, at the end of each day, the children and parents were told about the food to be provided the next day.

These small, but intentional, routines and structures (and also forewarning) helped the children to settle, relax and have fun. The children loved the playscheme. I know that, for the cohort of children we had, repeating the routine, and the foreknowledge for the next day (such as food, or if the staff was changing), helped them to feel safe and enabled them to relax and be able to play.

Recognising the areas of a trigger or conflict

With some of the children we work with, we recognise that there are key transitions that they find difficult and will always find difficult. When we know and understand this, we can adapt the day to support them. I discuss below some areas where we regularly use this in our work.

Arrivals and leaving

Arriving and leaving are often triggers for many children, especially in a setting where all the children arrive and leave at the same time. I talked about prewarnings and using visuals above. These are important, but for some children this is not enough. When everyone arrives or leaves at the same time, this often causes a lot of noise and movement, which can be overwhelming. A question to ask is: 'Can the child arrive or leave at a slightly different time to everyone else?' 'Or can they arrive and leave from a different place, which is quieter?' Some of the children I work with arrive 10 minutes later than everyone else, while others arrive at the main reception area and are met by their teaching assistant instead of at the classroom door. These small adaptations make the difference between a good transition for the child rather than a bad, distressing one.

Lining up

Many schools love the idea of lining up. I have to be honest, I don't understand this, and am not convinced it is a crucial skill for 4-year-olds. However, certainly in schools, it is used a lot. Most of the children I work with find lining up extremely difficult. Some can only cope with it if they are at the front of the line, while others can tolerate it for about a minute. My suggestion re lining up is to ask first if it is always necessary. If it is, make adaptations for the child who finds it hard. You could: give them another job, so they avoid lining up; give them a job and then get them to join the line just before it moves on; or have the child at the start of the line, with you supporting them. Either way, try to keep it to a minimum.

Mealtimes in big groups

This is less of an issue in early years settings, although some nurseries are very large and have a dining-room set-up that resembles that of a school. Mealtimes can be a tricky time for many children, especially if there are sensory issues around food, textures, smells, tastes and/or noise. They can be a great social time, with children and staff sitting together and eating. I think staff and children eating together is a very positive move and an excellent way of modelling eating and social skills to children. However, some children find mealtimes troublesome. It is worth considering the noise levels in the space. Think back to Chapter 5, on the environment. Is there a way you can soften the sounds? Maybe with material? Sitting with the child to support them is helpful and can be reassuring, but also think about what it is they are finding hard. If you know there are certain foods they cannot tolerate, don't give them those foods. If they do not like foods touching each other, serve their meal so this does not happen. If you know being with lots of people at mealtimes is hard, consider if there is somewhere the child can sit and have their meal with maybe one or two others, on the side of everyone else. Finally, it may be such a trigger for some children that the best way forward is for them to eat their food in a separate space with an adult and maybe one other child. The question all the time needs to be: 'What is in the best interest of this child?' If mealtimes are a hugely fractious time, making it hard for everyone, then you need to think creatively and find some ways around this.

Conclusion

So often we can take for granted the number of transitions and changes we expect a child to experience. It can be easy for us to disregard that this might be challenging for some of the children we work with. Sometimes we just don't realise how many transitions we expect the child to deal with during a day and, if we stop to count them, this number can come as a bit of a surprise. With all of these examples, the focus is on helping to prepare the child. As I mentioned at the start of the chapter, for some children lots of changes can be a challenge, but by using the simple tools discussed above we can help to prepare them in a step-by-step way. Many of the ideas I have suggested are simple, as well as good early years practice. Sometimes we just need to remember to be consistent in using them or re-evaluate how they might assist certain children we have in our setting.

 Further information and references

Early Learning HQ (2021) Visual Timetables and Routines. Available at www.earlylearninghq.org.uk/class-management/visual-timetables-and-routines/

Grimmer, T. (2018) *School Readiness and the Characteristics of Effective Learning: The Essential Guide for Early Years Practitioners*. London: Jessica Kingsley.

Little Owls Resources (2021) Personal, Social and Emotional Development. Available at https://littleowlsresources.com/psed

Mainstone-Cotton, S. (2020) *Supporting Young Children Through Change and Everyday Transitions: Practical Strategies for Practitioners and Parents*. London: Jessica Kingsley.

Payne , K. (2020) Supporting Children with SEND. Available at www.kathybrodie.com/articles/early-years-tv/ (members only).

Twinkl (2021) Visual Timetables and Routine –Visual Timetables. Available at www.twinkl.co.uk/resources/communication-speech-language-and-communication-areas-of-need-primary-send-inclusion-teaching-resources/specialeducationalneeds-sen-cognition-and-learning-visual-resources/visual-timetables-visual-timetables-and-routine-social-emotional-and-mental-health-difficulties-sen

7 Recognising feelings and emotions

If I was to identify one key thing that parents should focus on teaching their young children, it would be helping them to recognise and understand their feelings and emotions. We adults often presume that children understand that they are happy or sad, angry and worried, but how can they if they haven't been taught from a young age what this means? We see many examples of adults who have limited understanding of their emotions and feelings, and in Chapter 4 I discussed how adults need to be self-aware and to have this emotional vocabulary and understanding. Throughout this book, I have mentioned how young children are not able to self-regulate and they need to be taught the skills to do this. An essential part of teaching, and the modelling of self-regulation to children, is to help them know and understand their feelings and emotions. This can start at babyhood.

How we start with babies and toddlers

As mentioned earlier, we need to ensure we use emotionally rich vocabulary with children right from when they are babies. When a baby cries because they need changing, we can pick them up and acknowledge how they are feeling: 'You are really sad because you need changing. Let's go and change you now and make you more comfortable.' When they are hungry, again we can acknowledge this with our words: 'Wow, you are cross because you are so hungry. I'm going to feed you now.' A newborn baby will not understand the words we are using, but they will know they have been listened to and responded to in a caring way, and over time they will begin to learn what the words mean. When they are toddlers and they stop in the middle of the pathway and cry and flail in despair as they cannot walk any further, the adult can stoop down and say, 'Oh, you are feeling so fed up, I think your little legs are tired and you have had enough.' If we continue to name and recognise the emotions and feelings with children right from the outset, we are beginning to offer them the words and understanding about how they are feeling and to help them to know it is OK. I am always delighted when I hear a 3-year-old tell me I am cross or shout in despair that my legs are tired. This shows me they have an excellent start in gaining an emotionally rich understanding and vocabulary.

Taking judgements away from feelings and emotions

So often we place judgements on feelings and emotions, and this is particularly relevant for children with SEMH needs. I know 3- and 4-year-olds who have already been labelled the 'naughty boy', 'demon child' or 'difficult child'. These are strong labels and ones I would never use, but I have heard them from parents and professionals. These labels are making judgements about the child, based on the strong feelings and emotions the child feels and displays. I have also had children aged 3 and 4 tell me themselves that they are a 'naughty boy' or 'bad child'. I had one little boy tell me after he'd been dysregulated and upset that he was a 'bad boy'. This is tragic and upsetting and comes from judgements we make around feelings and emotions. It is so important as adults that we help children from a young age to understand that feeling angry or upset or jealous is OK; that the feelings and emotions are not bad or wrong. Of course, this does not mean it is acceptable to hit, bite or hurt others when we have strong feelings, but we can help children to understand this without making them feel shamed or like a failure. For many of the children I work with, these labels (and stories attached to a child) are a huge concern, and can stay with them. Often these labels and stories arise because people have not taken the time to wonder and be curious about what is going on for the child and why they might be communicating in the way they are. Instead, they have made a judgement and swiftly labelled the child.

TAKE A MOMENT

How comfortable are you with strong feelings?

Adults often portray their difficulties to children. Just for a moment, think how comfortable you are with your own feelings and emotions? Here are some things you might want to consider:

▶ How do you feel about being angry or when others are angry?
▶ Do you recognise when you feel jealous?
▶ Do you recognise the feeling of joy, and experience this?
▶ Do you ever feel despair or a sense of hopelessness?

It can sometimes be helpful to think about the labels we put around our feelings. Some of us grew up believing that anger, irritation or rage should not be expressed and we were wrong to feel these emotions. The feelings themselves are not wrong and it's very healthy to be able to recognise these in ourselves, but of course we have responsibility over how we respond to them. As mentioned in Chapter 4, Brené Brown (2021) has explored this area a lot, and has written many excellent books on the subject. I would recommend you look at her work.

It is helpful for us to be able to reflect on how we respond to feelings and emotions. Some people naturally want to avoid strong emotions and they can find it challenging, and sometimes threatening, when they encounter them in a child. When working with children, we must have a good level of self-awareness, know what we find difficult and understand what our personal triggers may be. We will all respond to emotions and behaviours differently. I worked with one member of staff who really couldn't cope with spitting, which made her furious. Unfortunately, that year we had a little boy who would regularly do so. Being able to have a conversation as a staff team about our reactions and how we all felt was so helpful – together, we were able to plan a strategy on supporting staff and the spitting child. When I started working with children with social, emotional and mental health (SEMH) needs, it was angry outbursts that I found difficult. My reaction to extreme anger is to step away, but in my role that is often not possible or appropriate. Years on, I feel calmer about this. I have learned to take a deep breath – sometimes stepping away is the right reaction – but I can now sit and be with the angry person, notice, be vigilant. I don't always feel the need to escape. It helped me to know and understand how I was reacting.

Tools we can use

The rest of this chapter discusses a variety of practical ways we can help children to develop a rich understanding of feelings and emotions. I will share many of the games, activities and resources we have found useful in the team.

Feelings boards (aged 2 plus)

Many settings use these with children when they arrive at a setting. They are also used to capture when a child feels a change as the day progresses.

You will need

▶ a board with each child's photo laminated with Velcro or Blu Tack on the back
▶ laminated images of a range of different emotions.

As they arrive, get each child to put their face against a feeling on the board. If you are using this kind of resource, it is important that the key person looks at the photos, notices what feeling the child has chosen and then checks in with the child about this. Again, if children are encouraged to change the board during the day, staff must notice this and act on it.

Circle time (aged 3 plus)

Many settings use circle time at some point in the day. It is an excellent opportunity to explore feelings and emotions. This could be through using stories, singing and also resources about feeling and emotions (such as picture cards or games). Here are some ways to do this.

Have a range of feelings faces, and get the children to choose one and hold it in front of them. You will need enough faces for everyone to do this or take it in turns. Do not insist that children talk about the chosen feeling unless they want to, but you could say something like, 'Would anyone like to tell me about the feeling stone/picture/cushion they are holding?' Staff need to take part in this, modelling emotional vocabulary to the children.

The range of great resources has increased – including feelings pebbles, cushions, soft toys, pictures, posters and cards. You could spend a fortune on these, but you really don't need to. Make your own pictures, using photographs of the children displaying a range of feelings. You could also gather some pebbles and draw feelings faces on the pebbles, or make feelings wooden spoons, with faces drawn on the back of the spoons. At the end of the chapter, I list some of the companies I like for these resources, including a company called Elsa (2021), which makes very cheap resources you can download.

Feelings dolls

Some settings have feelings dolls and soft toys available for children to use when they need them. Some children like to hug these or talk to them when they are experiencing strong feelings, these can be used in circle time as well as throughout the day. I have a worry monster keyring, as well as a bigger worry monster soft toy that often gets used (Sense Toys 2021). Some children like to hold these and talk to them when they are feeling sad, worried or cross.

Books and songs linked to feelings and emotions

There are a growing number of books for children linked to feelings and emotions. I have listed a few I like and use a lot (see 'Further information and references').

Two of the songs and rhymes I really like are 'If you're happy and you know it' and 'Cry, cry when you're sad' (also see Preschool Express 2021).

Emotion resources (aged 3 plus)

As well as the large number of emotion books on the market, there are also a growing number of resources available. I have already mentioned emotion pebbles and cushions above, but here are some other resources I have used.

Emotion fan

You can make your own or buy one. This is similar to the visuals I mentioned in Chapter 6. These can be used as a visual aid to talk to a child about their feelings at a particular moment.

Emotion dice

These have a range of different emotion faces on them. Use them as a game: roll the dice and see which emotion appears, then get the child to name it or act it out. The Elsa website (2021) provides some templates so you can make your own.

Emotion snap/bingo/dominoes

You can buy these or make your own.

Emotion board games and puzzles

There are a variety you can buy, but most of the games on the market are aimed at children aged 6 plus.

Emotion flashcards

I have a set of cards by the author Todd Parr (2010) that link to a book he has written (which I like and use a lot). These cards are great, as they cover a wide range of emotions. There are 20 cards, each of which has two sides/two emotions – for example, 'happy'/'sad', 'worried'/'carefree', 'disgusted'/'delighted', 'excited'/'disappointed' – and each side has the word and a colourful image to accompany it.

These cards can be used in many ways. With younger children, I use a few cards and see if the child can find me a picture of (say) 'happy', 'sad', 'angry', and we then talk about the pictures. With an older child, I use a few of the cards and we talk about the word and the picture – for example, with 'disappointed', I might say, 'I wonder why the boy is disappointed' (the picture shows a boy holding an ice cream which has fallen, and he is crying). With a child who has a greater understanding and vocabulary, I would get them to find me a card and tell me what is going on, how the person is feeling and what the story is. You can use these and adapt them in many ways. We have also found they work for younger children, but older primary children enjoy them, too.

With all of these resources, it is about using a range of tools and having the conversations. Talking about how we are feeling continues every day, throughout the day.

Mirrors (babies)

Mirrors are perfect for modelling and showing children emotions, and for practising emotion faces. Naming and showing children an emotion in the mirror is a lovely, fun activity that babies and toddlers adore. Show them a smiling face: 'Look, I am smiling, I am feeling happy.' Or 'Look, I am frowning. I feel cross.' Or 'Look, my face is looking down. I am feeling sad.'

As the child gets older, make a copying game with the mirror. Get the child to pull a face, then you guess what the feeling is and copy it. Take turns.

Music and art (aged 3 plus)

Using the arts to help children think about how things make them feel can be a lovely activity. When they were younger I used to play this regularly in the car with my daughters.

Play a piece of music, or just a section, and ask the child how it made them feel. Did it give them a feeling inside their body? For example, did it make them feel bouncy and happy and wanting to dance, or did it make them feel slow and sleepy and calm?

The same goes for pieces of art. My husband is an artist, so our girls grew up going to art galleries, right from when they were babies. We would often stand and look at a piece of art and talk about it, asking them how it made them feel. Did it make them sad or angry, or worried, or maybe they felt happy when they looked at it? Some may think this is the kind of activity you would do more with an older child, but it works just as well with younger children.

Linking emotions to the feelings inside us

Many children find this very tricky. They might have the words for happy, sad and angry and possibly other emotions, but linking the words to the feelings inside them can be harder. A lot of emotion resources talk about the emotion, but don't always link this with how it actually feels inside. Pixar's *Inside Out* (2015) helped to move this conversation on, so we talk more about what is going on in our body and head. I love this film and use its characters a lot in my work. It is more suitable for children aged 4 and over.

Other resources specifically link feelings inside our body to emotions, such as those by Learn Well (2020), a small company in the United Kingdom. They have a range of resources that work well at helping children to understand feelings inside their body, featuring pictures and words on cards. For example:

- feeling fizzy in your tummy, you have a big smile, your heart is beating fast, you want to jump or flap or clap – excited
- feeling that you might explode inside, you are scowling, your heart is pounding, you want to stomp or kick – angry

> feeling restful inside, your breathing is slow, your face is resting, you are still – relaxed.

Last year, I made a resource for the school to use with one little boy. This child had some strong emotions, but was unable to recognise and link the feelings inside his body to the emotion. He loved animals, so I made some pictures of animals and talked about the feelings inside, and also had a toy animal to go with each picture. The staff used the pictures to talk to him about his feelings and emotions – it's just one of the tools that assist them. It worked for him and, after a few months, he was able to say, 'I feel jumpy inside like a frog', 'I am worried' or 'I am cross and snappy like a crocodile today'. This won't work for some children, but the key is working out the right resource for each child.

The pictures and examples I had were:

My heart feels jumpy like a frog. [worried]
My tummy feels like it has a bee buzzing in it. [anxious]
Inside I feel like a snappy/bitey crocodile. [angry]
Inside I have big whale feelings, I want to get away. [flight]
Inside I feel still and frozen like a seal on a rock. [frozen]

The Elsa website (2021) also has resources that link emotions to feelings inside our body. This useful website is developed by a group of educational psychologists. Many teaching assistants in school are Elsa-trained. I like their resources, although some of them are more suitable for older primary-aged children.

Script

As well as all the above resources and tools, the other essential (and underpinning) part of our practice is using a script. The idea of using a script is that all the adults use the same words to support the child. These words are about recognising the feelings and emotions the child is experiencing. The main idea for a script is to keep it simple, don't use too many words, be consistent with it. With the children I support I introduce using a script at the start of the work. I and all the adults in school working with the child and parents all use the same script. The words in a script recognise what is happening for a child, it validates those feelings but also sets some boundaries if that is needed. The main phrases I use in most of my work are:

I am wondering if you are feeling cross. It's OK to be cross, but it is not OK to hurt me.

I am wondering if you are feeling mad. It's OK to be mad. I am here to keep you safe.

Other examples you might use are:

It's really fine to feel [emotion], but it's not OK to [action].
I'm still here. I'm still OK. It's going to be OK.
I am here to help you.
I am here for you.
I'm with you.

Interview with Sharon Cooke

Above, I shared some of the tools we can make, buy and use to embed an emotional vocabulary and understanding into the everyday. Now I am going to interview Sharon Cooke, who is one of our team. Sharon shares some of the creative strategies she uses to help children to think about their emotions and feelings.

Sharon, can you tell us about some of the ways you help children understand their feelings and emotions?

The first thing is, one size doesn't fit all. It's about knowing the child really well. There are four things that I think are important: visual illustrations, vocabulary, activities to hang feelings on, thinking about body sensations and recognising the body sensation so the child can verbalise.

The first thing I do is use a balloon if they like balloons. I blow a balloon up and let it go, and as it whizzes around the room, I say, 'Oh, that is what happy looks like.' Then, when it is down on the floor all saggy, I say, 'That is what sad looks like.' Then I blow it up again and let the air out slowly and it makes the screaming noise. I say, 'That is scared.' It might come out quickly or it might a bit slower, depending on how scared. Then I blow it again, and I keep blowing, and keep blowing, until it bursts (if the child can go there), or we just imagine it bursting and I say, 'That is angry.'

Then I would revisit the four basic emotions and I would do a particular activity and a book so they can hang the feeling of 'Oh, this is what it feels like when I am happy/sad/ scared/angry.' I would do things like bubbles, balloon games, pass the parcel. While we do those, I would talk about the grade of feelings – for example, being happy, but how that can go into being excited? I also bring in colours and ask, 'If happy was a colour, what colour would happy be?' And then we would think about how they feel. Are they warm or are they cold? We talk about where they feel it in their body, trying to think about 'I am feeling really warm in here [pointing to their chest].'

I know you use books a lot in your work. How do you mix these with activities?

I have books which I like to use which deal with all the different emotions. It gives them a situation based on an emotion. It tells them what the body sensation is and what it might look like and how they might behave, and then it gives them practical ideas. [See a list of these books at the end of the chapter.]

I try and do something that links to the story, so for 'sad' I would have three biscuits and share them. We both have one, but for the last one I talk about how they would feel if I had the second biscuit and they didn't. We would talk about how it makes them feel and link it back to the balloon we did before and the colour they thought of before.

For 'angry', I like to make popcorn. We talk about how, sometimes when we are angry, we get hot and feel in a spin – we get hotter and hotter until we explode. We watch the popcorn in the popcorn-maker doing this and then we eat the popcorn. We then talk about what we can do to calm down before we explode. We talk about breathing and I might show them some breathing exercises or we talk about sitting and having a cold drink of water, and how that can slow us down and help us to feel calmer. We also talk about climbing and how, when we are climbing, we need to think really carefully about what we are doing. We also talk about chewing on something hard. All of these are ideas that might help them to feel calmer, and we try them out.

For 'scared', I would have a mini pretend campfire and we would sit and drink hot chocolate and talk about things that make us scared. I would talk about levels of being scared, so I might say that I am bit scared of earwigs. 'I am scared of the dark, but I am terrified of tarantulas.' It helps them to see there is grading and a difference. I would then link it back to the balloon, the colour they chose and the feeling inside their body.

Once children have begun to show a basic understanding of emotions and feelings, how do you help them to develop this?

When the children can cope more with the feelings, I would do games that involved taking turns, waiting and choosing, and we would talk about the feelings they were experiencing during this.

I found using colours very useful. Some children find it hard to say they are feeling angry or happy, but they can relate to colour. I use the car emotion pack with some children. This is a resource from Elsa Support [2021]. The children have a laminated picture of different coloured cars and, when they arrive in from playtime or arrive in the morning, they park a coloured car picture on the emotion they are feeling. There is a laminated sheet with different colours/ emotion cars in a car park. This then shows the staff how the child is feeling without them having to use words. The staff can see they have come in from play and they have put their car on red. They are feeling angry, which is an indicator to state they need to support the child, find out what is happening for them. It also has a scale with it – so, as children begin to understand their feelings, you can ask them to measure their feeling: 'How angry are you feeling – a 1, which is a bit miffed, or up to a 5, which is really mad?'

Feelings games

In addition to Sharon's ideas above, I use some other games and activities trhat are linked to emotion and feelings.

Abracadabra

Tell the children you are going to 'magic' them into a feeling. When they hear the feeling word, they show you how it looks. Use the word 'Abracadabra' (or your own word) and 'magic' the children as they stand in a space to laugh/become cross/frown/ shiver/look hot/look excited/look sad. Try different emotions and feelings for the children to try.

Playdough faces

This works when a child is calm and has some emotional understanding and vocabulary.

You will need

- playdough
- googly eyes
- buttons for noses
- pipe cleaner or sticks for mouth

Ask the children to make faces. Talk about the faces you have made and how the children are feeling. To extend this, you could ask the child what has happened for the face to feel like that.

Biscuit faces

You will need

- digestive biscuits
- icing pens
- edible eyes

Ask the children to decorate the biscuits as a face. As above with the playdough, talk about the feeling they have made, and why the face feels like that. Then eat the biscuits and talk about the texture, the taste, the smell. Ask the children how they feel eating it.

Nature faces

You will need

- card cut into the shape of a face
- glue stick
- collect petals/leaves/twigs, etc.

As above with the playdough and biscuits, this is about making faces with petals and leaves, etc. You can use a face-shaped card to put them on, or you could draw the shape of a face outside in the sand or on the soil.

Ideally, get the children to collect flower petals and leaves, etc. to make the face, and talk about the face when it is made.

Make a happy book

Draw or stick pictures in the book of things that make them happy. When they are feeling sad or need to find some calm, they could look at this.

Social stories

In Chapter 6, I wrote about using social stories to help children understand a change that is happening, such as moving to school or moving house. We also use social stories to help a child understand feelings and emotions. I have written a variety of social stories, some of which were based on feelings and linked to a character the child enjoys. In the past, I have written one based on *Thomas the Tank Engine* characters and *Cars* (2006)from the Pixar film. I have used images of the characters and written feeling words about them. Here is an example from the Pixar *Cars* story:

> Mater has arrived to be in a race, he thinks it will be funny to race his friends. He is laughing.
> Lightning likes racing, it makes him feel very happy.
> Finn thinks he is the best-looking car, he feels very proud of his blue paintwork.
> Holley is confident she will win the race, she knows she is fast.
> Rod is feeling angry, another car said unkind words about his colour.

Another way I use social stories is around a specific issue. One child I worked with was unkind in the words he used to adults and children. I wrote a simple story based on a hedgehog called Percy. Here is an example from the story 'We Speak Kindly to People':

> This is Percy the hedgehog.
> Most of the time Percy feels happy and uses kind words and a kind voice to his friends and family.
> But sometimes Percy's voice sounds very cross and shouty and his words are mean and unkind.
> Sometimes Percy shouts to his mummy: 'GO AND GET ME SOME FOOD' or, to his friends, 'GIVE ME THAT TOY' or 'I HATE YOU.'

When he sounds mean and shouty, he looks cross and his friends can feel a bit scared. His mummy and friends feel sad when Percy uses mean words and an unkind voice.

Percy does not want to make his friends and family sad. Percy does not want to scare his friends and family. Percy starts to practise using a kinder voice. Percy starts to practise saying kind words. What are some kind words Percy can say?

Social stories are quick and easy to make. I write them on the computer, and put an image linked to the story on each page and a few sentences. I print them off and laminate them and we use them in school and at home. There are many books we can buy to support children's emotional development, but sometimes we need something so specific it is easier and cheaper to make our own. I would encourage everyone to have a go.

Conclusion

We can begin to use emotion language with children from babyhood, by embedding it (alongside emotion games and emotion activities) in our work and in our homes. This is what gives children the important tools they can use throughout their life. We always need to match our ideas to where the child is, so if they are having a day where they are really struggling and finding everything hard, then an activity such as making playdough faces may not work, whereas the popcorn idea mentioned by Sharon in her interview might be perfect. Also, wherever possible, a positive way to help the child engage is always to bring in their interests. One year, I worked with a little boy who adored My Little Pony®, so these were included in everything we did, from trying out sensory play activities to pony books about emotions and feelings. As adults, we need to be curious about a child's feelings and emotions, and creative in the ways we can help them to understand them. There is no one tool or programme of work that will work with all children, so we need to be creative and adaptable, planning our work and tools around the needs of the individual child.

Further information and references

Brown, B. (2021) List of Core Emotions. Available at https://brenebrown.com
/downloads/

Butterfield [Harvey], M. (XXXX) *Everybody Feels …* Stafford, UK: QED
Publications.

Cars (2006) [film] Emeryville, CA: Pixar Animation Studios.

Early Years Resources (2021) PSHE Feelings and Emotions. Available at www
.earlyyearsresources.co.uk/pshe-c52/emotions-c117

Elsa Support (2021) Managing Strong Feelings Resources. Available at www
.elsa-support.co.uk

Inside Out (2015) [film] Emeryville, CA: Pixar Animation Studios.

Karst, P. (2000) *The Invisible String*. Los Angeles: DeVorss & Company.

Learn Well (2020) Emotions Resources. Available at www.learnwell.co.uk

Llenas, A. (2016) *The Colour Monster: A. Pop-Up Book*. London: Templar.

Moroney, T. (XXXX) *When I am Feeling …* Fitzroy, VIC: Five Mile Press.

Parr, T. (2005) *The Feelings Book*. New York: Little, Brown.

Parr, T. (2010) *Feelings Flashcards*. San Francisco, CA: Chronicle Books.

Percival, T. (2018) *Ruby's Worry*. London: Bloomsbury.

Percival, T. (2019) *Ravi's Roar*. London: Bloomsbury.

Preschool Express (2021) Music & Rhyme Station: Feelings Songs. Available
at www.preschoolexpress.com/music-station09/feelings-songs-april.shtml

Sense Toys (2021) Anxiety & Worries. Available at www.sensetoys.com/so
cial-emotional-skills-c35/anxiety-worries-c41

Tinkertray (2019) Tinker Tray Play. Available at www.tinkertrayplay.co.uk

Witek, J. (2013) In *My Heart: A Book of Feelings*. New York. Abrams
Appleseed.

8 | Sensory experiences

Sensory experiences are one of the underpinning tools we offer in our role as nurture workers, along with using an emotionally rich vocabulary. Many children arrive in Early Years settings and schools without having crucial sensory experiences through sensory play. For me, the deficit in sensory play opportunities comes about for a variety of reasons. There seems to be growing anxiety from some parents around their reluctance to engage in sensory play with children due to the mess it may cause. I can understand this, especially for families living in rented accommodation. Families can be worried about mess or damage they may cause or, for parents who find time is a very limited resource, the thought of spending ages cleaning up after play may be one chore too many for them. Another concern can be around dirt and germs: for some families, there is still high anxiety surrounding children playing in the mud or puddles. I still hear parents yelling at their child, 'That is dirty and will harm you' as the child is happily digging out a worm in a muddy puddle. In Chapter 9, I will explore further how being outside and playing in nature – playing with mud, sticks and finding beetles – has huge benefits for children!

I also wonder if there is a growing deficit in the knowledge of many parents around the importance of sensory play, and how sensory play is hugely beneficial to their children's brain development, emotional development and learning. Often sensory play is called 'messy play', but I stopped using this term many years ago, as I feel the name has negative connotations and does not help to encourage parents to engage with it. In the 1990s, with the rise of Sure Start centres and children's centres offering universal access across England, sensory play or messy play sessions were often part of the core offer to all families. This enabled families who didn't want the mess at home to be able to take their child to a free or very cheap session and allowed the child to have those important opportunities. Sadly, with the Conservative government in the UK stripping away funding from many children centres over the last decade or so, many children's centres have closed and those that remain rarely offer universal services. This has contributed to a deficit of vital early sensory experiences for children, I feel.

Why is sensory play important?

We know that using our senses is a crucial way to learn about and discover the world around us. We immediately think about the senses – sight, hearing, touch, taste and smell – but along with these are the interoceptive, vestibular and pro-prioceptive senses. The interoceptive sense links to our body's physical condition; whether we are hungry, thirsty or in pain. The vestibular and proprioceptive senses are also understood as the inner senses. The vestibular sense helps us to process information which relates to the pull of gravity –its receptors are located in the inner ear and are activated by changes in head position and movement. It helps us with senses around speed, balance, gravity and direction. The proprioceptive sense helps us have a sense of how our body is moving, such as sitting, lying or standing. The proprioceptive receptors are found in our muscles, tendons and joints. Engaging the proprioceptive sense can help a child to regulate. (I will share some ideas about this for later in the chapter; see also 'Further information and references'.)

Babies and toddlers naturally, and automatically, engage their senses: touch-ing, licking, putting things in their mouths, choosing to lie against different sur-faces, or holding on to things that vibrate, repeatedly rolling over and pulling themselves up. Sensory play can be both engaging and stimulating but also sooth-ing and calming, meeting both of these needs. Tracey Beckerleg (2008, who was a special needs teacher and portage worker, argues that sensory play can also:

▶ help with relaxing children's muscles
▶ support the development of fine and gross motor skills
▶ support social play, turn-taking and and sharing
▶ support communication skills and concentration skills.

Many of the children I work with find it extremely hard to concentrate on many activities, especially those that involve sitting and concentrating. They may man-age a few minutes but often not more, and are often the children who appear to flit from activity to activity. However, when they are given a sensory activity, they can often engage in this in an extended way that they rarely do with other activi-ties. We know that play is a crucial way in which children learn and develop, so if we take away one element of the play experience and opportunity, then we are minimising the chances for children in their ongoing learning. Hopefully, this chapter will uncover some of the ways we can embed sensory play and how helpful this will be to the children you work with.

Sensory play is for all children, not just Early Years ones

Many Early Years settings are excellent at offering sensory play opportunities, but this provision declines as children reach school. Reception classes offer some, but in my experience not enough, and once a child gets to Year 1 and above the opportunity for sensory play often disappears. This is unless the school has a Forest School on site or Forest School is embedded into their curriculum – sadly, this is not embedded in all primary schools. During the summer holidays, I was working on a playscheme for some of the more vulnerable children aged 4 to 11 in our area. The whole play scheme was based outside and full of sensory play opportunities. The highlight for many of the children was playing with clay and paint. For many of the children, across the ages, they didn't have an end project in mind, but they enjoyed the sensory exploration. There was one 11-year-old boy, who found it hard to concentrate and engage in school and could explode with frustration. One day he spent one and a half hours playing with clay and water – he didn't 'make' anything, but enjoyed exploring the texture, exploring what he could do with the clay and how it responded to different movements. When I asked him about it, he said, 'I just like the feel. I like how it makes me feel, calm and happy.' This was another reminder to me that sensory play is not just for Early Years children, but it benefits them all. I think it benefits many grown-ups, too: often adults choose to engage in different sensory experiences as a way of supporting their wellbeing. I knit and felt, and I also garden – these are all highy sensory experiences, which I find calming and soothing.

TAKE A MOMENT

Think for a moment about your own sensory input.

► What sensory activities do you find nurture your wellbeing?
► How often do you allow yourself to engage in these?
► Do you make time to fit these into your life regularly?

Think about the sensory opportunities you offer to the children you work with or in your family. Do you see these as being just for younger children? If so, are you able to extend them to older children, as well?

What happens when children don't have sensory play experiences?

We talk about nature-deficient children, but I believe we also need to recognise that some children are sensory deficient in the opportunities they have. Sadly, I fear this issue is growing in tandem with the increase in technology with young children. Many of us see children arriving at nursery who can swipe across a screen but don't know how to use playdough. We see children who will happily talk about a game they have played on their iPad, but are unsure what to do in a mud kitchen. As mentioned above, sensory play gives children opportunities to try out, experiment and be curious. Through sensory play, we can extend their language. Through sensory play, children have the opportunity to extend their fine and gross motor skills. They also develop their creativity and begin to wonder, ask questions- and explore. There is also an argument that early sensory play gives you the full bodied experience that equips you for later learning. For example, the fully immersive experience of doing body painting when you are 2 years old – when you get into the paint, notice the prints you have made with your body parts –then equips you for knowing how paint works when you are given a paintbrush as an older child. You already know how the paint feels, what it looks like and what you can do with it.

When there is a deficit in sensory experience, this can sometimes lead to children being fearful and anxious around sensory play. Each year I often have a child in my cohort who will be averse to getting their hands dirty, not wanting to touch certain textures – they become distressed at the idea of touching things. Not always, but sometimes, they have had no sensory play opportunities in the home and have chosen not to engage in them at nursery, so have had a very limited sensory experience. This can sometimes lead to anxiety feelings and behaviours. Or these children may be sensory averse and find the textures and experience disturbing. When children are frightened or alarmed by sensory experiences, we need to gently support them with this – for example, give them tools to poke the playdough with, rather than them having to use their hands. On the other hand, some children totally crave the sensory experience – they are sensory seeking most of the time. These are the children who will touch anything, endlessly put things into their mouths, stroke things or smell everything. These children will often head straight for the most sensory activity on offer in the provision and, if they can't find something, they will often create a sensory experience for themselves, such as making loud noises or tipping things out.

Diagnosed sensory difficulties

Some of the children will already have a diagnosis and a sensory difficulty may form part of that – for example, autism, sensory processing disorder, dyspraxia, attention deficit hyperactivity disorder (ADHD). However, many children we see in the Early Years won't have a diagnosis, and part of our role as Early Years practitioners is to be curious about what children are showing us. Sometimes we will go on to question if there is something further going on, but we also need to watch and notice how the child behaves around sensory experiences. Here are some useful questions to ask:

- ▶ Are they sensory seeking?
- ▶ Are they sensory avoiding?
- ▶ Does some sensory input help to calm them?
- ▶ Does some sensory input help to engage them?

If through our observations and conversations with parents, we think there is a high sensory need, we may need to seek advice from the SENCO and the area SENCO. We might also need to make referrals to an occupational therapist and/ or paediatrician.

Open-ended and non-prescriptive

One of the key reasons I think the sensory play works so well for children with SEMH needs is that it is open-ended. There is no right or wrong way to make this work; there are no prescribed answers or solutions. The child can freely play and explore – they cannot get it wrong. For the children I support, this is so important. So often, they are led to feel they get things wrong, but in the safe space of their nurture time within the play they can freely explore and investigate and be curious without having to 'make something' or achieve something. This is especially important in schools, as so much of the work there is about achieving something. Children know this and can find this challenging. Some people think that an adult-initiated craft activity is sensory play. I don't agree with this. I think that is something different – it is using sensory materials, but I would not define it as sensory play. For me, an essential element of sensory play is the open-ended aspect of the play. therefore, if the child decides to make a finished product, such as a cat, with their playdough or clay, that is fine, but this is different from an adult saying, 'Today we are making a cat with clay.'

Different sensory experiences

As mentioned above, I view sensory play as opportunities to use sensory materials in an open-ended, child-led way. Lots of the work I do with children involves sensory play and later in this chapter I will share some activity ideas. This is the main part of my work at the beginning of the school year, when I first start working with a child. Their emotional needs are high, they need the space to safely explore, and to be curious and discover through sensory play. As I have mentioned in earlier chapters, our team use the Thrive assessment tool and plans. When we first start working with a child, we often work at their Being level, which meets their needs at 0 to 6 months.

The open-ended aspect of sensory play is crucial. I have found that, once a child has had many repeated opportunities to play with sensory rice, playdough, crazy soap, in water play, etc. (see below), they are then ready to move on to other types of sensory activities, but this foundation of sensory play is crucial. As mentioned in previous chapters, children with SEMH needs often go back to earlier development stages when they are in a situation where they feel unsafe and overwhelmed, this is where the sensory play can help to meet their needs. Just as a 6-month-old loves to play and explore with baked beans – running their hands through it, squashing it – a child of 5 or 7 (or older), who has gone back to the earlier developmental stages, may also want to be soothed or engaged in playing with couscous or rice or waterbeads.

Other sensory experiences that we often offer to children may be in a slightly more structured way. However, we only use these once a child has settled, once they have built a trusting relationship with an adult and are beginning to feel safe and can cope with following instruction or are able to try something new with the support of an adult. This more structured play follows on from the initial sensory play, and we begin to introduce other sensory experiences, such as making playdough together, making bread, making fruit smoothies and planting seeds.

As well as the sensory experiences that meet children's five main senses, we also use vestibular and proprioceptive sensory experiences. Sometimes we need to engage these first, before we move on to the other senses. If a child is in fight or flight, they may need some support to engage their proprioceptive sense. Using tools that help with the feeling of push and pull, or weighted support, can help them with their overwhelming feelings. For example, you could use a weighted blanket to wrap around a child if they are feeling overwhelmed, as this can help them to feel contained, safe and held. Or you may have a dog toy that you use to do a pulling exercise, with the child one end and the adult the other. Yoga activities can help in a similar way. I share more sensory activities for the vestibular and proprioceptive senses later on in the chapter.

The key with this is recognising where the child is at, and what is going to support them at that particular time, and this will change from moment to moment. All our work aims to fit to the individual needs, likes and dislikes of the child. We will have many ideas in our head as to what might work for the child, but (as with all good Early Years work) we need to be able to adapt and change in the moment if the child shows us they need something different.

Using sensory play and sensory breaks to support children emotionally

In schools, the idea of a sensory break has been increasingly recognised as an important way to support a struggling child. Rather than continuing to insist that the child sits and listens on the carpet, when they are clearly not managing to do that, an alternative idea is to offer them a sensory break. This can help to get them back into a place where they are ready to re-engage. Although sensory breaks are often used in schools, the idea can also be used in the Early Years. If we can see that a child is finding it hard to join in with everyone else, giving them a sensory break or a different opportunity may help them, and stop further difficulties occurring at that time. This might include: giving them something to fiddle with while they are in circle time, getting them to go and do a job (such as washing up the cups) while the rest of the group are talking about the weather or encouraging them to stand up and help with the actions of a song or action for the story.

TAKE A MOMENT

Early years settings are often excellent at offering sensory play, but how often do you think about sensory play in relation to supporting a child's emotional needs? If this is a new concept for you, spend some time as a team reflecting on this, thinking how you could incorporate sensory play.

Linking sensory play with emotions and feelings

In my opinion, sensory play, sensory activities and sensory breaks are the ideal way to integrate emotional language and understanding into our work. When we play with sensory materials, they naturally lend themselves to a conversation about how they feel, smell, look, taste and sound. This isn't about bombarding the child with questions, but as an adult you model the language, as you are play-ing with the child. This is crucial: children need adults alongside them who play along with them, not just watch. We need to be prepared to get our own hands dirty/sticky/wet, etc., through our play. We can make comments such as 'Ooh, that feels sticky – my fingers are sticking together. I quite like that feeling' or 'I feel calm when I am running my hands through the rice.' I will often comment on what a child is experiencing. If I have noticed they are calm while playing with something, I will tell them: 'I can see you are very calm while playing with the rice. Your face has softened and your shoulders have dropped. That is lovely to see.' Or perhaps: 'You seem so happy playing with the waterbeads. I love hearing your giggle of delight.'

As I mentioned in Chapter 7, children don't always know how they are feeling and what they are experiencing. It is just as important for us to remind them, and show them when they are feeling happy, calm or joyfu, and other positive feel-ings and emotions, as well as talking about the negative ones. Children who have SEMH needs are often told when they are cross or angry and overwhelmed, but we can forget to mention the positive emotions. If we continue to highlight these positives, in time the child will remember that the waterbeads made them happy or the rice helped them to feel calm. This will help them to develop their coping and managing strategies.

In Section I, I wrote about the experiences that many children with SEMH needs have experienced and how they often have a small window of tolerance. In Chapter 1, Nicky Spencer-Hutchings spoke about adults needing to 'turn the temperature down' for children, helping them get back to a safe space internally. Sensory play and sensory work with children are powerful tools that help children with this transition.

In the next part of the chapter, I share some resources that are useful for supporting children's sensory experiences and helping them when they become hyper- or hypoaroused. You can do these activities either inside or outside, whereas Chapter 9 discusses specific sensory activities that engage with nature and the outdoors.

Calm box (aged 3 plus)

When you are working with a child and you have identified that they have high sensory needs, I suggest you make them a calming box. This is the child's support box and not to be used by other children. You put things inside it that work for the individual child, so every box will be different.

Find a box, if possible a cardboard box with a lid. The first thing to do is to get the child to decorate it, so they feel they have ownership of it.

Here is a list of things you might put in the box, but (as I said above) it needs to work for the individual child.

▶ Tangle (this is a fiddle toy – great for twisting and turning and fiddling with)
▶ pipe cleaner (works in the same way as a Tangle)
▶ small pot of bubbles
▶ soft material (for rubbing between the fingers or smoothing against the skin)
▶ stress ball
▶ massage stick (for using on their arms or their back, over the child's clothing)
▶ small tin of Lego
▶ yoga cards (different poses you can try)
▶ playdough
▶ stretchy toy
▶ smelling bags (lavender/camomile/dried herbs)
▶ material (so they can cover their head/hide under it)
▶ calming bottle or discovery bottle
▶ windmill for blowing
▶ food, such as carrot sticks or a mint (this may sound odd, but if a child is hyperaroused, giving them something to crunch in their mouth can help to calm them; and if they are hypoaroused, eating a mint can help this – see Chapter 2 for more on hypo- and hyperarousal).

Safe space/tented space (age 3 plus)

As described in Chapter 5, a quiet space/tented area can be a sensory, soothing area for the child to be in. If you have created such an area for the child, it is worth putting the calming box (see above) in here, as it is another tool to support them.

Weighted blanket (age 4 plus)

Occupational therapists sometimes recommend these for children. A growing number of schools have them for specific children and find them very helpful. They used to be very expensive and you could only buy them from specialist providers. However, more people (parents, schools, workers) are hearing about them, and they have come down in price and can be bought from Amazon (or other online shops). Weighted blankets are useful for children who need additional sensory input. Having something heavy on them can help them to feel calmer and more safe. Both my daughters, who are in their twenties, have some sensory needs. They find that a weighted blanket helps them to feel grounded when life feels a bit overwhelming.

Useful sensory play ideas and activities

This section outlines a variety of sensory play ideas and activities that i use and find useful in my work. See the end of the chapter ('Further information'), where you can find other ideas.

Sensory rice (aged 3 plus)

This is my favourite calming play. Even with the most agitated, distressed child, I have found that sensory rice always calms them.

You will need

- ▶ 1 bag of rice
- ▶ children's ready-mix paint
- ▶ baking tray
- ▶ sealable tub.

Put the rice into a carrier bag (or similar), pour in some paint, then squash it around until it covers all the rice. Tip the rice on to a baking tray and air-dry for a few hours. Once it is dry, put the rice into the container. This keeps for years.

Children love to run their hands through the rice, exploring its texture. You can add toys to the rice. I often put lavender seeds in, to assist with a calming feeling and scent. I am not sure why, but this is the activity that seems to calm the most aggressive and agitated child. I once had a little girl who was deeply unhappy and self-harming, and we were struggling to find ways to help her. One day I offered her a tub of sensory rice. She immediately engaged and spent 20 minutes or so running her hands through the rice. Her shoulders relaxed, her face softened and she murmured, 'I love this.' In many ways that was a turning point for our work with her, because we found something that soothed her. I have found this with other children, too. There is something about the feel and the sound that appears to offer some calmness.

Waterbeads (aged 3 plus)

You will need

▶ 1 pack of waterbeads (or large couscous)
▶ sealable tub.

Waterbeads are one of those resources which you either love or hate, and are easy to buy online. They are tiny beads that you put into a bowl, submerge in water for a few hours and then watch them grow. Once they have grown to the size of a small marble, you can strain off the water and put the beads into a tub. I often put a few drops of lavender oil into the water to help assist with a calming smell and feel (as with the sensory rice above). They feel wet, but they are not wet play – it offers a curious sensation. Most children I work with love them and often giggle with delight at the feeling. I have found they are really useful to use with children who are withdrawn and maybe showing some frozen behaviours. In my experience, they work less well when a child is highly agitated: they have tipped the beads everywhere in agitation, and they are very bouncy, which makes retrieving the beads rather tricky! They are not to be used with children who put things in their mouth. Although it says they are non-toxic, I would not risk it. If you have a child who puts everything in their mouth, you can use large couscous pearls or tapioca instead (although personally, I find these pretty revolting!). It's all down to personal likes and dislikes.

Homemade playdough (aged 18 months plus)

Homemade playdough is such a stalwart of every Early Years setting that I am not going to put instructions here, but my favourite recipe is from the Imagination Tree website (2021). Playdough is wonderful for open-ended sensory play. It is great for a frustrated child, as they can knead and pummel and squeeze, which assists their proprioceptive sense and helps them to let go of their strong feelings. Once a child can cope with following instructions, then it's a lovely activity to get them making the playdough with you, which offers lots of opportunities for conversations about texture, scent and colour.

Along with playdough, I also like to make cloud dough. This is one part hair conditioner to two parts cornflour. Mix them together, and then play. It has a very soft feeling – it is slightly crumbly and, depending on the conditioner you use, can smell lovely. This mixture works less well for kneading and pummelling, as it breaks a bit more easily, but it is good for rolling and squashing.

Bubbles (from babies)

Bubbles are a regular feature in my work. I often use them for bubble breathing, which is a mindful activity (see more about this in Chapter 10). Bubble play also works well for open-ended, fully immersive play. Using bubbles is one of those sensory play ideas which attract most children of all ages. During the summer playscheme, most days we had big buckets of bubble mixture out, along with a variety of homemade wands and kitchen implements that could be used for wands, and there was often a child – 4-year-olds to 11-year-olds – playing with them. The combination of the sensory feel and watching the bubbles float away can be soothing and calming. Some of the older children commented they had forgotten how much they liked playing with bubbles.

Homemade giant bubble wand

See Inner Child Fun (2015) for how to make these. Giant bubbles are my favourites: children (and adults) delight in seeing the size of bubbles, and some love it when the bubbles go over their heads and they can stand right inside them.

Pipe cleaner wand

You will need

- ▶ pipe cleaners
- ▶ beads.

Make a loop at one end of the pipe cleaner and twist the end around the pipe cleaner to make a letter P. This makes the wand head. Put some beads on the other end of pipe cleaner – this makes the wand handle. Fold the end over to stop the beads from falling off. Then dip it into the bubble mixture and start to play.

Bubble snakes

You will need

- ▶ empty plastic drinks bottle
- ▶ scissors
- ▶ old sock.

Cut the end off the drinks bottle and cover the end with the sock. Then fold the sock over, leaving a gap at the mouthpiece of the bottle. Dip the sock end into the bubble mixture and blow through the mouthpiece. You will get a bubble snake coming out of the bottle.

Bubbles with your hands

Dip your hand into the bubble mixture and make a circle with your fingers, then gently blow through the circle.

Bubble mixture recipe

This is the bubble mixture recipe we all use in our team. It works especially well for giant bubbles, although you can use it in a small pot too. It also saves us money on buying endless bubble mixture!

- 6 cups water
- 1 cup strong washing-up liquid (eco ones don't work very well; Fairy Liquid does)
- 1 tablespoon glycerin (to give it strength).

Mix gently, pour into your pots, and get playing!

Crazy soap (aged 1 plus)

You can buy crazy soap in supermarkets, as well as online. It is soap in an aerosol can and looks a bit like shaving foam, but I prefer crazy soap, as it is mouldable. You squirt it out, in the same way you would shaving foam or squirty cream. All the children I work with love this sensory play. I have been using it this week with my new children, and it brought squeals of delight and pleasure from all of them (including a few who have been displaying frozen behaviours). This works well with children who are not keen on the mess, as it disappears quite quickly if they rub it into their hands or rub it over the surface. It also makes the most delightful noise when you squeeze it between your fingers!

Sensory tubs (from babies)

Sensory tubs can take many different forms. They are open-ended and link with a mixture of the senses. I often use sensory tubs in the first term, when I am first getting to know a child. If I know they have a particular interest, I will create a tub that fits with their interest. For example, I am currently planning a dinosaur tub with sand, bark, moss, wood shavings and dinosaurs for one of my new children. If you use these with younger children, then put things in the tub that are appropriate for their age. In many ways, these are similar to the heuristic play we do with babies and toddlers.

Here are some of the ones I like to use.

Autumn tub

Fill a box with leaves, conkers, acorns, beech nuts, sweet chestnuts. Sometimes I hide woodland animals in there, too: an owl, rabbit, deer, hedgehog, etc. If it is feasible, I get the children to help me collect the autumn leaves, etc. They love to rummage and explore, and you can use lots of emotion words in this play, noticing textures and smells. I often link this activity to the feeling of being a little bit nervous or scared about how something will feel – for example, a spiky conker shell.

Bug tub

Cook some spaghetti and then cover it with some sunflower oil and black food colouring. This looks and feels slimy! Put it into a bowl, and add toy bugs and worms to it. This play is fantastic for children who love things that feel slimy and gooey. Add other toys to it if you want to. This play also works well for children who put things in their mouths, as it is edible. Perhaps also add water to the bowl and see how that changes the feel of the mixture. This is a great activity for using lots of language around textures and how they make us feel.

Banging and smashing tub

Some children have so much pent-up feeling, and a good way to help them express this can be by banging and breaking things safely. I put some breakfast cereal into a tub – for example, Cheerios. I give the child a small hammer and invite them to see if they smash all the cereal. Sometimes they look a bit shocked, but often they love it. Before we start, I might say, 'I am wondering if you have lots of big feelings inside you and you need to get them out. This might help you.' We would then talk about how it is OK to smash up cereal, but it's not acceptable to break toys or hurt others.

Gloop

You will need

▶ 2 cups of cornflour to every 1 cup of water.

Mix the cornflour and water together. This is a regular favourite Early Years activity. It is a unique texture, as the mixture moves from solid to liquid. I like to make up a large batch of this, and sometimes add food colouring. This often becomes a fully immersive activity, with children having their full arms in it. I have even had children wanting to stand in it. For children who find sensory play difficult, this can be a challenge for them. One way to support them is to use toys in the gloop. This way, the child doesn't have to touch the gloop, but they could put a dinosaur or plastic animal into it. Then they could use spoons to rescue the toy, without having to touch it. I find that, over time, the child then feels able to try and touch it themselves. As the adult supporting this, I would always model and show the child how it feels. I would play with it, and they may just watch at first, before dipping their finger in.

Food play

Food often features in the work I do, and mostly this is linked to making and eating. I know there are some concerns in Early Years settings about using food in play, with understandable worries around culture and poverty: for some people playing with food is outside of their cultural norms; and for others it is very offensive to use food in play when some families do not have enough to eat. I would encourage you to think carefully about these issues when you are planning sensory food activities. I mainly use food in play if we can also eat it. Using food can be an excellent tool for thinking about the senses and our feelings. Also, some of the children I work with don't have enough food at home, so using food in our nurture sessions has become an important part of the session, enabling them to eat as well as exploring their senses. Here are some of the sensory activities I use that involve food.

Bread rolls (aged 3 plus)

I love making bread with children. It is very simple and wonderfully sensory. I find it works especially well with children who have strong emotions and feelings that often bubble over. The kneading, pummelling and stretching involved in making the bread meet the proprioceptive needs, and can help bring a child down if they are feeling agitated or angry. Making bread is sticky, and it also has a strong smell, giving loads of opportunities to notice how it feels and smells. Then, once the rolls are made and cooked, there is the lovely experience of eating them together and thinking about how it feels to eat warm, buttery bread (see Parker 2021 for this recipe, at the end of the chapter).

Fruit smoothies (aged 3 plus)

You will need

- different fruits
- blender
- knife
- chopping board
- cups.

This is often a favourite with the children I support, and every year one or two children tell me they don't like fruit. But they are often happy to explore different fruits, cut them up, maybe taste them as they are doing that, and most of them love putting the fruit into a blender and mixing it all up. If I think that the child can cope with it, I will try to introduce some new fruits they may not have tried before. I only use this activity once I know the child is in a calm place, when they can listen to and follow instructions. This is usually an activity I would do in term two or later.

The point with all of these food activities is for the child to have a high sensory input in a fun and enjoyable way. Therefore, if the adult is constantly warning them, holding them back, worried about any dangers, then the fun and enjoyable part disappears. Once we have made the smoothie, we then drink it and talk about the taste and smell, and how we feel about them. Sometimes children love the idea, but then really dislike the taste or look of the blended fruit. If this happens, that's OK – talk about how we all have different likes and dislikes, and suggest they may like some of the fruit on its own (it's worth keeping some back for this purpose).

Painted toast (aged 2 plus)

You will need

- toaster
- sliced white bread
- milk
- food colouring
- paintbrushes
- small pots.

This activity works well with children who are less keen on getting their hands sticky. First, make up some edible paint with milk and food colouring. Get the child to help you with this. Then share out pieces of bread and invite the child to paint a picture on the bread. I often ask them to paint something that makes them happy. Once they have finished the painting, we look at each other and notice the colours and what they have painted. Then we toast it. The picture stays on the toast – the children love this and find it very exciting – and then we eat the toast. In this activity, you use lots of emotion language and feelings.

Edible paint (from babies)

You will need

- ▶ natural yoghurt
- ▶ flavours to add (for example, yeast extract, honey, raspberries, blackberries).

Make up small pots of the paint using the yoghurt and added flavours. It is fun to do this with the child, talking about the smells and textures. Then invite them to paint with it. Do explain that this is not for taking home, as it will be a bit smelly in the end, but it is for playing and experimenting with. Some children only want to use paintbrushes or sticks with this activity, but others quickly put their hands in the paint and enjoy mark making with their hands. I like this sensory activity, as it works well across ages and abilities.

Water play (from babies)

Water play is often a sensory favourite for children. I have discovered, with several children I have worked with, that water play can soothe and calm them. It is not always possible for Reception classes always to have water play available. However, they often have a large sink area. One girl I worked with became increasingly agitated as the morning progressed, so we started to get her to do some washing up in the sink when she was becoming agitated. Every time this brought down her stress levels. She liked having a special job to do, as it helped her self-esteem, and it also met her sensory needs. There are many water play ideas available. A few that I use and enjoy are listed below.

Ice cubes

You will need

- ice cube trays
- variety of objects to put in them.

Fill ice cube containers with different objects, such as toys, flowers and leaves. Freeze them, then invite the child to explore with them. They might try melting the ice cubes or breaking them with a hammer. One little boy enjoyed doing this daily with his teaching asistant for months. This was his choice – through this play, he was experimenting, developing his ideas, and he enjoyed the familiarity of it. He continued to be delighted that it worked every time. At the start of the work, he was extremely agitated, but through the teaching assistant following his lead and interests, and safely enabling this play, he came to a place where he was calmer.

Ice chalk

You will need

- ice cube trays
- 2 cups cornflour
- 1 cup water liquid paint or food colouring.

Mix up the cornflour and water, then add the food colouring or paint. Pour the mixture into ice cube trays, and freeze. When they are frozen, use them to make marks on the path outside. At first, it will appear dull, but as the water dries, the colour becomes more vibrant.

Physical activities

As mentioned at the start of the chapter, our senses include vestibular and pro-prioceptive senses. These are ones many people don't think of as often, and when we think of sensory activities for calming, the physical activities may not be the first ones that come to mind. I have noticed that this is often the situation in schools, which can be good at offering calming boxes, but some children need a movement intervention first.

There have been two particular instances where I have worked with a couple of boys, and I needed to learn and listen to their vestibular and proprioceptive needs. Both of them were loudly telling and showing me and the staff what they needed. We needed to listen, notice and learn.

One boy had lots of angry outbursts and, after these, he would find a way to hang upside down. We began to realise this was an important release for him, and over time he was able to recognise the strong feelings and would request to hang upside down. At the beginning of Year 1, he walked around the school site with his headteacher and they agreed together on the safe spots where he could hang upside down. Another year I had a boy who, again, had many angry outbursts and the only thing he could cope with in those moments was playing tug-of-war on a dog pull toy. He would pull incredibly hard, with a member of staff on the other end, and sometimes this would last for 20 minutes or more. Only then would he begin to feel calmer. Within themselves, both these boys knew this helped them and they needed this.

Below are some movement interventions that can work well:

▶ bouncing on a mini or large trampoline
▶ bouncing on a space hopper
▶ climbing
▶ yoga moves
▶ racing up and down in a space
▶ hopping
▶ balancing
▶ skipping with a rope
▶ pushing a wheelbarrow with things in it
▶ pulling a rope
▶ hanging upside down.

Conclusion

It can be easy to overlook a child's sensory needs, especially if they don't have a diagnosis that states sensory needs. However, if we can stop to reflect on a child's sensory needs when we are carrying out our observations, and then offer some high-quality sensory input, we are hugely benefiting their wellbeing. Meeting a child's sensory needs can make a huge difference to their ability to be able to concentrate and to join in, and also to their overall wellbeing.

Further information and references

Abraham, D., Heffron, C., Braley, P. and Drobnjak, L. (2015) *Sensory Processing 101*. LLA Media LLC.

Beckerleg, T. (2008) *Ideas and Activities for Children with Special Needs*. London: Jessica Kingsley.

The Imagination Tree (2021) Available at https://theimaginationtree.com

Inner Child Fun (2015) How to Make Giant Bubble Wands. 5 May. Available at https://innerchildfun.com/2015/05/how-to-make-giant-bubble-wands.html

Parker, C. (2021) Easy 'Hedgehog' Bread Rolls Recipe for Toddlers and Preschoolers. 16 January. Available at https://rainydaymum.co.uk/hedgehog-bread/

9 Outdoors

We know that outdoor play is vitally important for children's wellbeing. And, for children with social, emotional and mental health (SEMH) needs, I think embedding a practice of being outdoors and being in nature is possibly one of the most positive things we can do. There is growing evidence that outdoor play opportunities and being in nature lower stress levels in children and adults. This has become especially clear to many people during the Covid-19 lockdowns, with many people using their daily walk and being in nature as an essential way to help their mental health. See 'Further information and references' for organisations that specialise in the connection between nature and mental health.

As I have discussed in earlier chapters, many children with additional SEMH needs experience high levels of cortisol, the stress hormone. Given the evidence that stress levels and the body benefit from nature, I believe we need to consider more ways of using the outdoors with children. This feels particularly important currently. During the time I wrote this book, in the UK children and adults experienced three lockdowns. Many children were out of school and nursery for around seven months. For many children, returning to school and nursery brought a mix of relief, excitement to see friends but also higher stress levels from the experience of lockdown and being out of their normal routine. One vital way to support children through this is by increasing their opportunities to be out in nature.

A growing number of books have been written on the importance of outdoor provision for the Early Years (Knight 2013; Louv 2005). In this chapter I'm going to consider how we can use outdoor spaces to help children with SEMH needs to engage, participate and thrive. Many of the children I work with have behaved and appeared very differently when in an outdoor space, especially woodland areas.

I've mentioned before the playscheme I was involved with during the 2020 summer holidays. All of the children who attended were identified as being vulnerable children, and a number of them had SEMH needs. Our playscheme was based outdoors for the whole time, in a woodland area of an infant school. The children had the opportunity to play freely, make dens and get involved in making a treehouse. My role was to support their emotional development. Given that many of them hadn't been with other children throughout lockdown, and a number of them hadn't been outside, I was slightly worried how they would be, emotionally, during our time together. Fortunately, I didn't need to worry, as the children engaged and were emotionally calm and happy for the entire playscheme.

Many of these children ordinarily have teaching assistants in school to support them, or work in small groups as they struggle with the large class. Part of the positive experience for them was that we were not making any education demands on them; it was a free-play setup, following children's interests. However, I have no doubt what helped the children to be so calm was the experience of being outside and the opportunity to be surrounded by trees, to be outside in all weather (and we did have heavy rain at times). The fully immersive outdoor experience was so enriching and nurturing for these children, and it was very moving to see and be part of the experience. I've been a great believer in outdoor learning and the benefits of nature for a long time, but for me this playscheme took it to another level. Not only did the children find this an enriching and hugely positive input to their wellbeing, but it had a huge impact on staff, as well. We anticipated being exhausted by the end of the two weeks – generally running a playscheme is very tiring for the staff. But this was different. Instead, I think we all felt totally alive, and had a new sense of joy and wellbeing that none of us were expecting.

Disconnection from the outdoors

There is an increasing fear that children are getting disconnected from nature, and are spending a lot of time inside and have limited opportunities to be outside. Richard Louv's (2005) *Last Child in the Woods* has been hugely influential to many people, helping many adults to compare how much time they spent outside when they were children with how much time their own children or grandchildren do so. These concerns are still prevalent more than 15 years later. Within the Early Years, a growing number of settings are choosing to follow a Forest School approach (Knight 2013). This has been enabled since Bridgwater & Taunton College developed a BTech in Forest School in 1995, which was inspired by practices they had seen in Denmark. I love the Forest School approach, and have been influenced by it in my work, but I am aware that for some settings this can feel impossible when they don't have a woodland area near (or as part of) their provision.

I have been encouraged to see more and more ideas and suggestions as to how settings can embrace the outdoors, even without a woodland area. For example, Kimberly Smith has set up Hygge in the Early Years (see 'Further information and references'). As part of this, she has a 52-week training programme to download (Wanderlust Child Nature Study programme), in which she encourages staff to help children engage with the natural world. Kimberly recognises that many children and adults in the United Kingdom have little connection with nature, often not knowing the names of wildflowers, trees or the wildlife surrounding them. Through her course she offers ideas, suggestions for open-ended resources and information sheets for staff to use as support in their practice. I like Kimberly's course, as it offers every Early Years practitioner a way in to help their children engage more in nature. For many staff, this feels more accessible than the idea of training to be a Forest School teacher or feeling put off because they don't have woodland provision around them. I also enjoy the way she brings noticing and mindfulness outside into her approach.

How the outdoors supports emotional development

For many children a key difference between being outdoors and indoors is a sense of space: they often feel less confined and have space to move freely. A child once told me, 'I feel like I can breathe properly when I am outside. When I am inside, I feel like my heart might explode.' We can especially see this with a child who is feeling overwhelmed or dysregulated. When I can see a child I am working with is beginning to fizz, I will try to get them to go outside, as this will often be enough to stop the escalation.

For many children, part of the pleasure of being outdoors is the chance to do and engage without getting it wrong. Many of the children we work with in our team have low self-esteem: they often presume they can't do things, and fear they will make a mistake. Often the outside environment does not put the strain or constraint on them that they feel inside. I frequenty see children physically changing when they spend time outside: their shoulders lower, they appear to stand higher, they begin to smile more and generally look more relaxed. The outdoor learning environment also often encourages child-initiated learning, enabling them to be curious and learn at their own pace about what fascinates them.

131

During the playscheme, one 4-year-old boy was fascinated by digging trenches. Each day he dug more of his trench. At times, other children and adults joined him, and he would instruct them and direct them about what to do. He investigated adding water, noticing how the water flowed and what depth the trench needed to be to collect water. He experimented to see if adding clay into the trench would help to keep the water in (it didn't!). This little boy continued with this play and investigation for eight days, during which we observed him using mathematical skills, science questioning, partnership working, problem-solving, not to mention a rich vocabulary. He demonstrated early engineering and leadership skills to us, and this was fantastic to see. In class, he hates work – he doesn't want to do Maths, he flits, he finds it hard to concentrate – but outside, he was motivated, inspired and focused. His wellbeing was high, he was in the flow and deeply absorbed.

Attention and focus

The outdoor environment often encourages focus and attention. As mentioned above, this can be hard for many children indoors, especially so for those with additional SEMH needs. However, when we are outdoors, and help children to stop and notice and engage with a sense of awe, wonder and curiosity, this supports a child's ability to notice. But, for this to happen we need adults who also have a sense of awe, wonder and curiosity. We know that very young children have this in abundance, with their questions and their ability to stop and discover the tiniest of ants and insects on a pathway. Sadly, some children seem to lose this as they get older, and many adults seem to have lost it completely. If we want children to have curiosity and an interest in the outdoors, as practitioners we need to actively encourage this. Rather than seeing the outdoors as a space to let off steam, we must view it as a nurturing, supportive space that encourages curiosity, exploration and investigation. We need to model this with children, if this is to happen.

TAKE A MOMENT

- ▶ When you are outside, do you look around with wonder and curiosity?
- ▶ When was the last time you spent time watching the leaves moving in the wind or watching a bee moving from flower to flower?
- ▶ How connected are you to nature?

> ▶ Do you know the names of trees and flowers, and different varieties of birds?
>
> ▶ Other than blackberries, do you know what food you can forage and safely eat?

If we are concerned about children losing connection with nature, we first need to look at ourselves and question how connected we are ourselves. My trip to Denmark around 10 years ago hugely challenged my own practice and engagement with nature. After watching children forage through woods and know what was OK (or not) to eat, and hearing them tell me the names of plants and trees, I realised that I had become disconnected from nature in my local area – I foraged for blackberries, and knew the names of a few trees and plants, but not many.

On my return to the United Kingdom, I set about changing that. I am extremely fortunate that I live in a rural location, and have a community meadow behind my house. Over the last decade or so, I have learned tree and plant varieties for the area I live in. I now know that we have three different varieties of wild orchid growing in the meadow, along with many other wildflowers, and around 15 different varieties of moths and butterflies in our garden and the meadow. I forage for food almost all year, knowing the different plants that are safe to eat and where to find them. I take joy in stopping and watching the buzzards fly on the thermals, and just this year we have had a red kite that flies over the village. During the lockdown, I discovered we have a family of tawny owls living at the bottom of the meadow. Even as I write this, the thoughts of these fill me with a sense of joy and delight. This is something I share with the children I work with. And, as I plan and think about my new school year and the nine new children I will be supporting, I am looking forward to sharing awe and wonder moments and experiences with them .

The attention we give to the outdoor environment

In Chapter 5, I wrote about the environment and how it can impact a child. Earlier in this chapter, I discussed how being in nature can support our wellbeing and reduce our stress levels (both children and adults). Nature is also an amazing sensory-rich environment, with so many textures, smells, colours and different surfaces. However, we need to think just as carefully about the environment we provide outside as the indoor environment. Although I firmly believe outdoor spaces are mostly fantastic, I have also experienced many outdoor areas for children that are far from nurturing, sensory and inviting. I must admit I have a particular pet hate of artificial grass. Although I know many settings choose this for ease and convenience – it can be used all year around – I find it uninviting, sterile and as far away from nature and sensory-positive experiences as is possible. I don't believe you need a large budget to provide an excellent and sensory-enriching outdoor space. Examples of free or very cheap resources are wooden logs, tyres, stones of different sizes, pots with herbs and grasses, pots with flowers, an area for digging, guttering, buckets to collect water, and various vessels to collect and explore with. These all enhance an outdoor space, providing a rich variety of sensory experiences and inviting child-initiated play, exploration and curiosity. If possible, I would also add an area for children to hide in – even better if it is child-sized. I know this can sometimes cause concern, because adults may not be able to see the children, but if you have risk assessed this well it can hugely enhance an outdoor space and a child's experience of it.

TAKE A MOMENT

Go into your outdoor space – if possible, as a staff team and without children. Spend some time noticing the environment. How sensory rich is this space? Think about the natural resources you have available and ask yourself:

- ▶ Is there a variety of textures to feel?
- ▶ Is there a variety of surfaces to walk on or climb on?
- ▶ Are there opportunities for digging?
- ▶ Is there a range of colours?
- ▶ Is there a variety of smells?
- ▶ What can you hear in the garden?
- ▶ What can you see in the garden?
- ▶ Is there wildlife in the garden?
- ▶ Are there ways you can enrich this space, to enable it to encourage more nature sensory opportunities?

Once you have looked at the space as a staff team, I would also encourage you to observe the children in the space. Notice what they are drawn to, what risks they can take in their outdoor play, and observe whether (and how) they respond differently outside to inside. Look at the way they respond to the environment using their senses. When you observe the children, pay particular attention to those with additional needs, and SEMH needs. Consider how they respond to the outdoor space. Is this different from the way they respond indoors? It is a good idea to speak to all the children about the outdoor space – find out what they think, and get them to take photos of what they enjoy and what they like doing. All of this information can assist you in planning, or changes you might want to make.

Sensory and emotional experiences outdoors

In Chapters 7 and 8, I wrote about ways we can support children's emotional development through the activities and play we perform. The outdoor environment is excellent for supporting sensory and emotional play. It naturally lends itself to high sensory input for children and, through this, is ideal for emotion language and conversations.

In the next part of the chapter, I share some ideas on how we can use the outdoors to support a child's emotional and sensory wellbeing. I also outline some of my preferred play and activities.

Bubble play (aged 2 plus)

You will need

- bubble mixture
- bubble wands

I wrote about bubble play in Chapter 8. This is an activity I use all year round. If you use bubbles when it has been raining, you will notice they land on the ground and stay in bubble form for several minutes, sometimes even longer. On an icy day, the bubbles form as mini ice bubbles. Blowing bubbles on a windy day is also an exciting and exhilarating play opportunity.

Ice creation (aged 2 plus)

You will need

- containers of different shapes and sizes
- water
- found objects from nature

On icy days, it is fun to experiment with collecting leaves and petals (if you can find them). Then put them into sand moulds in a tray or different-shaped vessel. You could put some string in them and leave them overnight to freeze. The next day, discover the frozen creations – if they have string in them, tie them together to make a mobile on a tree branch.

In Chapter 8, I wrote about waterbeads. It can be fun putting these in a container with water and then freezing them. For some children who find it hard to recognise feelings and the experience of hot and cold, ice play can develop these feelings and an ability to recognise what it feels like safely. Perhaps, use ice cubes and then have a bowl of warm water for them to put their hands or feet in. This shows them the contrast and to notice how the body reacts.

Fully immersion in leaves and snow (from babies)

You will need

- pile of autumn leaves
- snow
- all-weather outdoor coat, trousers and wellies

If you have full outdoor suits and wellies for children, it can be delightful enabling them to be fully immersive in fallen leaves or snow. They can lie on their back, making leaf or snow angels, noticing the sound and feel of the textures under them, thinking about how it makes them feel inside.

Nature soup or perfume (aged 2 plus)

You will need

- containers of different sizes
- spoons
- natural objects

Using a bucket or container, collect petals and leaves, find a stick to stir and add water. This is a common play activity that many young children engage in, and the use of mud kitchens in outdoor provisions encourages this. We can help children in this play to notice the smells and textures, and explore how it makes them feel. When we play with them in this way – and they have made us conker soup, for example – we can comment on how warm it makes us feel inside our body when we eat it, we can describe the warm sensation as we swallow it and we can tell them how happy we felt that they made us soup. Take the child's lead, but also scaffold and support the language of feelings and emotions.

Awe and wonder walks (aged 18 months plus)

You will need

- postcard-sized piece of card
- double-sided sticky tape

This is something I use with children when they can slow down and notice. I give them a piece of card with double-sided sticky tape on it. I explain we are going to explore and see what we can find and we can put our discoveries on the card. All the children I have worked with have loved this. Some have an idea and only want to find green things, while others decide only to put leaves on it, and others decide to find tiny petals. This is an open-ended activity, it doesn't have to look like anything, and children can add whatever they want. One little boy only wanted sticks on his card, while another wanted a conker and we then spent some time problem solving how to make the conker stick and stay on the card. This activity works best when we go slow and notice. I often use it as mindful activity. (More of these ideas will be shared in Chapter 10.)

Plant printing (aged 2 plus)

You will need

- flower petals
- leaves
- berries
- pebble
- white material
- chopping board
- paper

This is a fantastic activity. I only discovered very recently, at the summer play-scheme. Put the white material on the chopping board, then place the petals, leaves and berries on top of it. Cover these with paper and then bang each petal and leaf with the pebble. When you start to see the print coming through on the paper, it will be also be printed on the material. Lift the paper off and see your creation. This is a satisfying activity, and use the proprioceptive senses along with sight, smell and hearing. Children love it. It is also a great activity if someone is feeling cross, as they can let out all those strong feelings with the pounding.

Obstacle courses (aged 18 months plus)

Many of the children I work with love to make these. They can develop in what-ever way they want, using branches of trees to go under or logs to balance on or pots from the mud kitchen to carry things in. Obstacle courses are fantastic for supporting the vestibular and proprioceptive senses, encouraging the child to navigate different surfaces and physical movements. When I do obstacle course with children, it is not about having a race or challenge, but about using our bodies in different ways, using the range of our senses. I always join in with the children and do the obstacle course they have created. This always brings delight and communal laughter, when I find it hard to balance or duck low under a tree or climb a tree.

Planting (aged 2 plus)

During the spring term – when the children I am working with have usually reached a calmer and mostly more regulated place – we will do some planting. This is an activity to do when the child is more able to follow instructions and can cope with not having an immediate outcome, as plants take a while to grow! Many nurseries grow plants with children. I like doing the same with them, as it meets so many sensory needs: digging in the soil, getting their hands into the soil, using water. I feel there is also something positive about how it encourages a child to nurture something; to water it and check up on it. Many of the children I work with respond so positively to this, and when the plant grows they take such pride in how it grows and showing others. Of course, for this to work the children need staff who are going to support the child in the watering, etc. Sometimes it won't work: the plants get overwatered or underwatered or eaten by a slug. This inevitably brings some upset and disappointment, but they can try again, and this can support their resilience and emotional development. If you are not a gardener, I would suggest planting sunflower or calendula (an orange flower) seeds and, if you want to grow some food, peas can grow well. All these seeds are easy to grow, however, and are a good size for children to hold, plant and see. All of them grow in pots as well as in the ground.

In the next part of this chapter, I interview Andy Hattersley. She is part of our team and a trained Forest School leader.

 Interview with Andy Hattersley

Andy, we have all experienced that many of the children we work with are so different when they are outdoors compared to indoors. I was wondering what your thoughts are about that?

There are so many sections to this: the sensory aspect, the awe and won-der, the transitional. It's a place where they can feel free and safe to explore and to feel comfortable and relaxed and can learn as they go along. With Forest School, there is so much repetition to what we do and then we expand on it each time. It's so child-centred, which is brilliant, so for a child who is feeling that they are not special they can have something focused on them and their enjoyment; that session can build on that enjoyment. This is meeting their needs on many different levels. You can tailor-make each session to the child's individual needs, so it's not too big. Nature is such a place that is so full of awe and wonder. A lot of the children we work with don't have the opportunities or experience of being outside – they may live in flats, they don't have the space to explore outside, and often they don't realise there is a wealth of amazing things around them that are outside. For some children, they instantly take to it; some you have to draw their atten-tion to it and be curious with them and walk through it with them. Then suddenly it's almost as if you have opened up an Aladdin's cave to them, they are so full of 'Wow'.

Can you give us an example of how you have seen a child develop outdoors?

There is one little boy that I worked with. He came out, a bit reluctant; he sat down, looked around and didn't really get it. He was a bit anxious about being in a woodland, a bit anxious about the idea of getting messy. His anxiety levels were quite high, but over the time of being out in nature and learning to relish it, we could see his anxiety levels beginning to drop. He started to talk about all things he found – all the curiosity things, shells he found; he started to notice and enjoy listening to the wind. The sensory element of being outside calmed and soothed him and being able to explore and feel comfortable doing that. It hits so many areas we talk about in our nurture work and thrive about feeling safe, and if you feel safe you will want to explore and then you are ready to learn and become independent. We know there is lots of research talking about how healing nature can be, therapeutic and boosts our wellbeing. I have noticed being outside centred him. For the children that are unsure, anxious and have a lot of challenges, you see this dissipate over time as they become immersed in the natural world. It's very visceral because you are immersed in this natural world they feel on so many different levels, and this stays with them. For a child who is anxious and struggles to concentrate and learn, by being in a safe environment where they are calm and enjoying the space, you see the learning coming on in leaps and bounds. Nature does the work for us – we facilitate, but it's the natural world that does the teaching.

We have often heard from children in the classroom children saying they can't do it, but outside they seem more willing to give things a go. What is your thinking about that?

I think it is freedom. Sometimes they feel like they are pent up, caged up, when they are inside. I describe the outdoors as the classroom without walls, so often in the inside classroom they often feel like there are expectations to get things right, whereas outside they become so engaged by their senses they often don't have time to get into a panic about what they can or can't do. They often naturally start to explore and engaging. It also allows their body to use their proprioceptive senses, by swinging, climbing, running, hiding, going down a mudslide or being in a hammock. When they can do these things, we can start to see their learning take place, because their bodies are regulated and because they are being soothed by nature. Also, when they are outside, there are so many things they can manage and achieve quickly. They find a feather and you tell them that's amazing; that makes them feel good. Also, often when they are outside there is no set outcome and it feels play-based. You get to see the growth outside that you might not see in the classroom. Maybe in the classroom there are more restrictions; more pressure with the ideas of having to sit on the carpet, following what is being taught, lots of transitions and structure.

I think your comment about transitions is really interesting. You are right there are not so many transitions when they are outside, so that immediately feels less threatening.

In Forest School, we always set up manageable learning and tasks that they can achieve and immediate outcome, but in more formalised learning there is often ongoing learning. With the children we work with who have low self-esteem, or they struggle to concentrate, achieving something quickly makes a big difference to them. Just picking up a piece of paper and making a bark rubbing, they have achieved something immediately; making a mud pie they show you, and you delight in it, they feel good. Also, I have noticed that they speak so much more when they are out in the natural world. Sometimes inside they are not sure when to speak or not to speak, or they might be anxious and their voices are not being heard. I have one child I am working with at the moment who is Polish. His TA [teaching assistant] has said how much more he is speaking when he is outside; he is motivated by what he is doing and feels less inhibited to speak. This week we were den building. He was making a rope swing and he was saying enthusiastically, 'But look – it's a washing line, too.' His TA commented that when he is outside he is now starting to speak in sentences, which they are not hearing inside the classroom. His friends were then applauding him, so he was getting positive feedback, boosting his self-esteem.

We have also seen that being outside helps them to feel part of a community, feel part of the group in a way they often don't inside. I have one child in my forest group who finds it difficult to give positive feedback to other children or to be empathic and share. One week we were making bug houses. He found he was good at this and he was proud of it. He then felt able to extend this and he told me he had found so many woodlice he was sharing them out with other children, as they didn't have so many. He was able to tell the other children how good their bug homes were and was able to help them. Also, I have noticed that, sitting around a fire, children often feel more able to sit and chat. It isn't formalised – there are no correct answers to give, it's just talking. I have a few children with selective mutism, and around the fire they relax and feel more able to say things.

A huge part of all my sessions is play in nature. It is just awesome for children and is the biggest part of the attraction, connection and learning, as they just get to play and explore. In a more formalised learning environment, especially as children get older, the chance just to play becomes a lesser part of the curriculum. Through play, they learn so much more, develop their creativity. Their imaginations become fired up and they can just experience uninhibited joy. One boy of 5 didn't engage with imaginary play at all. As we know, this can sometimes be a challenge for children with SEMH needs, as this area can be underdeveloped. This was until he played at Forest School. He played different games in the woods, started feeling safe and confident, and then it really went up a notch when we were wizards and made our own wands, potions and did a short drama play about wizards in the woods. His teachers noticed this child entering into far more play in the playground, accessing games, developing social skills and made huge progress in his literacy and storytelling. Also, he smiled lots more, too!

Can you finish by giving us some of the outdoor nurture activities you enjoy doing?

This year I have given each of my children a small wooden hedgehog and they needed to make a home for the hedgehog. This was a very sensory experience, as they needed to collect the sticks, find some moss, find leaves and make the house. We had conversations about why they have chosen something: it might remind them of a blanket they have, or they like the feel of it. It's encouraging them to look after something – they feel like what they are doing is special for their hedgehog. They each made a house. One child made a house with two floors! The sensory aspect of touching different textures, and the nurturing aspect of taking care of something and keeping it safe, is wonderful for them.

We often make dens, using lots of different materials. They enjoy wrapping themselves, using different fabrics. One child put my leafy net over his head. He sat in the middle of the grass and was covered in this leafy net – he was calm and happy.

[Mud painting] is always very popular. I get them to dig for the mud (looking at it, feeling it and noticing it), then sometimes we add powder paints, or other times we add natural dyes. We might use berries – for example, blackberries – and get them to crush them with a pestle and mortar, and we crush leaves to get the natural juices out. They mix this with the mud. I take paper for them to use, smaller and bigger pieces. The beauty of this is that we can extend it in many different ways. I have used paper and canvas. Sometimes they like flicking the paint over the canvas or paper; other times they do handprints; sometimes this moves on to prints on to logs and bark. Others

use sticks and other natural things to use as a paintbrush. It can extend in the way the child wants to take it. This is great, as it can go from small to big, and they love that development.

We often make playdough, but I experiment with adding different things – for example, seaweed powder, herbs, spices. They can add leaves and sticks into this and develop it in many different ways.

We take [water play] in many different ways. I bought some cheap guttering – they were working out how to make a slide, what would slide quickly and slowly, putting their hands under it and catching the water, seeing what can slide and move. This is highly sensory, and fun.

They love hammocks. I have my own that I bring in, or sometimes we use a large piece of material. If you are a bit worried about what you have strung the hammock to, you can have two adults holding each end. They often find the hammock really soothing, being gently rocked.

[Spider webs] are always very popular. You can make a small one on sticks, where you bind sticks together and they loop the string around and around. Or you can do it on a bigger scale, where they make one in a tree, wrapping the string over the lower branches. Some children are so engrossed in this, they can spend ages making this web. Sometimes they then join them to other trees.

[Bug hunting] is a gift that keeps on giving. They love it, being able to go off and explore, find and look for the bugs. Then you can make a shelter for the bugs and it can keep extending. We often repeat this, as you find different things. It is teaching them about awe and wonder and the natural habitats, and how to take care of the wildlife, and it is so sensory.

[Bark rubbing] is lovely, as they are feeling and smelling. It is so easy to do and can be quick. We know that smelling bark releases chemicals which make us feel good.

[Storytelling] incites so many sensory explorations, wondering what is behind the door and who it belongs to. We sometimes make potions for the fairy or a wand, so it meets sensory play and imaginative play.

I have also noticed that being outdoors and embracing the seasons can really help children think about change. Noticing the changing seasons can help them realise change can be good, and linking the changes in nature to other changes, and understand it doesn't have to be scary.

Here are details of the outdoor nurture activities Andy mentions in the interview above.

Home for creatures

You will need

- small wooden hedgehog
- sticks
- moss
- leaves

Den making

You will need

- material
- string
- trees or branches to hand them from

Mud painting

You will need

- mud
- small spade (for digging)
- paper
- sticks

Playdough

You will need (see Brand 2020 for recipe)

- flour
- water
- oil
- cream of tartar
- spices

Water play

You will need

- water
- vessels
- guttering

Hammock

You will need

- hammock (or large piece material)
- clips or rope

Spider webs

You will need

- string
- sticks or branches

Bug hunting

You will need

- magnifying glass
- pot or jam jar (with air holes)

Bark rubbing

You will need

- paper
- crayons

Storytelling

You will need

▶ little wooden doors (bought or handmade), to lean against a tree

---

TAKE A MOMENT

There are so many ideas here from Andy about how the outdoors boosts wellbeing for all children, but especially those with additional SEMH needs. After reading the ideas in this chapter, and before you move on, take a moment. Consider if there are any ideas you could try out with the children you work alongside.

Conclusion

I hope this chapter has given you some new thoughts and ideas for how nature and the outdoors can support children's wellbeing, as well as ways you can use sensory play to support children. These ideas will work for all children, of course, not just those with SEMH needs. Spending more time outside and in nature benefits everyone.

 Further information and references

Brand, L. (2020) *The Joy Journal for Magical Everyday Play: Easy Activities & Creative Craft for Kids and Their Grown-ups*. London: Bluebird/Macmillan.

Coles, J. (2016) How Nature is Good for Our Health and Happiness. Available at www.bbc.co.uk/earth/story/20160420-how-nature-is-good-for-our-health-and-happiness

Hygge in the Early Years (2021) Hygge in the Early Years. Available at www.hyggeintheearlyyears.co.uk

Knight, S. (2013) *Forest School and Outdoor Learning in the Early Years*, 2nd edition. London: SAGE Publications.

Louv, R. (2005) *Last Child in the Woods: Saving Our Children from Nature-Deficit Disorder*. London: Workman Publishing.

Mind (2021) How Can Nature Benefit My Mental Health? Available at www.mind.org.uk/information-support/tips-for-everyday-living/nature-and-mental-health/how-nature-benefits-mental-health/

10 | Mindfulness

The value of teaching children mindfulness has become increasingly known in the last few years, and many schools in the United Kingdom now use mindfulness practice in their classrooms. The charity Mindfulness in Schools Project (MiSP; 2021) has been delivering mindfulness training. It is linked with the Oxford University MYRIAD Project (2008–2021), which is researching the impact of mindfulness on children (see 'Further information and references'). Mindfulness is a tool that can help children and adults to stop, take notice, be aware of what is going on in their bodies and in their minds, and all around them.

So many of us live busy lives, rushing around constantly, and we can often become stuck in our heads, with many thoughts, worries and plans swirling around. When we live like this, we can miss the wonder and beauty, the small and simple, precious moments around us. In many ways, young children are fantastic at mindfulness, because they are naturally curious and interested and so often want to stop and notice. Sadly, however, our busy adult lives sometimes contribute towards knocking a young child's mindful, noticing character out of them. I believe we need to support this intentionally and nurture this aspect in children. Mindfulness helps us to notice and be more aware, but it can also help to support emotional regulation. When we are aware that our heart is racing, that we are feeling jittery, it helps us to stop, focus on our breath, notice what is happening in our body. It can help us to slow down our heart rate, to calm us.

I am a big advocate of mindfulness, and I have found it hugely beneficial to use the practice in my own life, but it does come with a warning. Some people have been traumatised by the act of stopping, focusing on their breathing, noticing what is happening in their body, closing their eyes, which can act as triggers for them. They will find it a frightening experience, not a calming one. It's important that we are aware of this. I never insist that someone closes their eyes, and I have found that for some people using mindful movement is better. Yoga is also an excellent way to help adults and children to be mindful, in a slow, active way.

The movement and breathing of yoga can feel less triggering and frightening (see Guber and Kalish 2005).

Mindfulness can be traced back to ancient Buddhist, Hindu, Christian, Islamic and Judaism routes – look back at all these religions, and you can find examples of this kind of practice. However, the mindfulness that is widely practised in the United Kingdom these days is a secular-based practice.

When they hear the term 'mindfulness', a lot of people think of sitting and meditating, and will often wonder how that fits in with the Early Years. This chapter does exactly that: it gives you a variety of ways in which mindfulness can work with Early Years children, and I share how you can use it in your practice with children. Many of these do not involve sitting still!

Children, silence and slowing down

I am concerned that we are creating a world for children which is often noisy and busy, one where life can feel fast and full. Many people seem to have fallen into the trap of feeling that adults' role is to entertain and stimulate children. For me, this is unhelpful for all children, but especially so for children who have social, emotional and mental health (SEMH) needs. Over the last 10 years, I have been exploring ways we can change that idea and why we need to do so. In Chapter 9, I wrote about a trip I made to a Danish preschool. On that trip, I observed a young girl lying on her back in an empty water trough, in her own peaceful space, just being still for around 20 minutes. As I watched her, I noticed that the staff were happy for her to be in her own space, having some time out, and the other children left her to just be. As I sat and observed her, I was impressed by how calm she looked. I realised I was watching a child who was enjoying some quiet time and it made me ask myself, 'When was the last time I saw a child doing that and being given the space to do that?' I also questioned when I last stopped and breathed and enjoyed the space around me. The image of the child still sits in my mind – that moment was pivotal for me. I recognised that I needed to learn how to slow down, to stop and notice and enjoy, to find a time to just be in the moment and find some calmness. I also knew that we need to help children find a way to do this.

Since that time in Denmark, I have explored ways to help children to experience stillness and a more unrushed way of being, and this has become even more relevant when working with children with SEMH needs. In earlier chapters, I explored the fact that many children who have experienced trauma, disruption and fear experience their minds and bodies to be in overdrive a lot of the time. We must help them to find ways to find calmness and peace, and provide them with the tools to do so. The longer I work with children with SEMH needs, I become increasingly aware that teaching mindful practice is an essential life skill and tool for these children.

Helping a child to recognise the feelings in their body

In the last few chapters, I have highlighted the need for children to be able to identify their emotions and how this feels in their body, and how we can support them with this. One of the important skills is to be aware of when we need some calm and peacefulness. Our bodies are amazing – they tell us when we need some space, calm and time to relax – but we need to learn to tune into our bodies and understand what is happening. If we don't see it in ourselves as adults, then it can be difficult to go on to recognise it in children.

TAKE A MOMENT

▶ How do you know when you need to relax? What happens in your body?
▶ Think about one of the children you work with. How do you know when they need to experience some calmness?

We adults know that if we constantly spend our lives being busy, filling our lives with activities, rarely stopping and slowing down, this will potentially lead to burnout. In Chapter 12, I focus on adult wellbeing and ways we can support ourselves (which is vital). But we need to teach this to children as well. We all know how fractious and unhappy children (and adults!) can become when they don't get enough sleep, or when they become overstimulated and overwhelmed. As adults, we need to be mindful of this and feel comfortable in adapting and changing our plans – sometimes to provide more stimulation, and other times to provide less stimulation and more calm opportunities. Many of the best teachers and nursery practitioners I work with are those who have a wide range of different activities to use with children, both when they are lethargic and floppy and need waking up and when they are overly excited and need support in coming down. These are all part of the regulation tools we use to support children. Regulation is not just around helping a child who is in a temper, but also around supporting a child who is lethargic or overly bouncy.

Case study

One little boy I work with often escalates quite quickly in his excitement and behaviours. He is never violent or aggressive, but can become hugely overexcited and overactive. Once he starts heading this way, he finds it extremely difficult to calm down and he needs support in this. If he does not calm, this can escalate to such an extent that he ends up accidentally breaking something, hurting someone and often getting into trouble.

If we are observant, we know when it is heading towards escalation when he:

- flits very quickly between activities
- becomes louder and louder and his voice gets higher in pitch
- starts to run in circles, his arms flailing
- begins to bump into others and knock things over, as he finds it hard to slow down.

These are just a few warning signs that he needs help with slowing and becoming more present. How many times have you seen this happening? I know I see this often, particularly in the last term of the nursery. Of course, there is nothing wrong with being excited, but sometimes it can bubble up so much it can become overwhelming and can all go wrong. Sometimes when a child is overexcited these feelings can lead to a sense of being out of control, just as a tantrum or rage can lead to these feelings. This can be a frightening experience for the child and others around them.

When we can see this happening, there are a few strategies we can use. Sometimes we get him to go outside and make some big movements, racing, or pushing or hanging, or climbing, similar to the proprioceptive ideas I shared in Chapter8, or we might make an obstacle course, giving him something to focus on. This type of focused and active exercise is in itself very mindful: it takes concentration, and it requires all your attention and focus. Remember: mindfulness is about being present, noticing and being in the moment. We can do this through activity – it does not have to be just about stopping and sitting.

When we can see he needs some help becoming more aware of what is going on, we use these words from our script: 'I can see you are excited and fizzing inside. Let's do some mindful things. What would you like to choose?' We also have some images that we use to show him some of the mindful options. By using the script, we are helping him to recognise what is going in his body, we are noticing and validating (but not judging) and we are supporting him to choose something that might help him.

Once we have done some of the more active things (mentioned above), we might move on to a more calming activity, such as bubble breathing or barefoot walking (I describe these activities later in the chapter). We also use language during these activities to help him understand what is happening in his body. For example, 'I can see your heart is working really fast as you push that wheelbarrow. Can you feel your heart beating? And your breathing is quite fast.' Then when we do a slower activity. We would say, 'Your breathing is slower now. That is helping your heart to slow down, too. Can you feel it is slower? This is helping you to feel calmer.'

Nature and mindfulness

In Chapter 9, I discussed how important it is that we enable children and ourselves to connect with the outdoors and how supportive this can be to our emotional wellbeing. I find that being outside immediately helps me to become more mindful. The very act of stepping into my garden or walking in the local field helps me to notice, to become more aware. I think it is the sensory element that helps me to be more mindful – to move out of my busy brain and to become aware of what is around me – and this in turn helps me to feel calmer. I have also experienced this with many of the children I work with, when they become overwhelmed, frazzled by the feelings in their body and their overactive mind. If we can get them outside, this often acts as an antidote to the place they were in beforehand. I am writing this chapter it is September, and this week I have been writing plans for all the children I support. In each plan there is an emphasis on getting outside, using barefoot walking, connecting with nature, as a way to help bring them some balance and sensory input from nature. See Davy (2019) for a beautiful book that discusses many examples of mindfulness in nature.

Mindfulness and movement

During lockdown I found it hard to sit and do mindful meditation, they just didn't work for me, whereas in the past they had done so. I mentioned earlier that throughout lockdown I did a daily sunrise walk to replace my morning swim, and this became an incredibly important and mindful act for me. In the early morning, there are deer, hares, rabbits and owls in the fields surrounding my house, but to notice them I had to be slow and silent. This act of slowing down, stopping and watching for the wildlife around, and looking at the sunrise, was very powerful. I became aware that it moved me from an anxious mind to a sense of calm and freedom. During lockdown, I found the main way I experienced this calmness was when I was outside on these walks. I have now returned to swimming, and this currently clashes with the sun rising, but in a few weeks the sun will rise when I return from my swim, and I plan to reinstate the sunrise walk. I have a feeling this will become crucial during the autumn and winter months.

We do not always encourage or nurture young children's natural sense of wonder and mindfulness, their ability to stop and notice. I would encourage you to think about how you can use your time outside with children to embed this into your practice. If you notice a caterpillar or a bug, stop and watch it, notice it with the children, share the wonder of what you are seeing. Or, if it's a blue-sky day with white clouds, lie on your back with the children and watch the clouds, notice how quickly they are moving and take on board the different shapes you can see. This is mindfulness.

Tools to help children through life

Helping children to be mindful and teaching them some simple life tools are crucial skills we can give to our children. We know there has been a serious rise in mental health difficulties with children and young people, and we want to be able to equip them with tools that become embedded and can be used throughout their life. I know primary and secondary schools are doing more to teach these, but it would be so much better if we could teach these skills to younger children, because they then have them in their toolbox for life. Stewart and Braun (2017) and Kinder (2019) both offer mindfulness activities and ideas to use with children.

For the rest of this chapter, I am going to share different mindful activities you can use with children. Some require you to be still and others involve movement. They could all be used outside as well as indoors, and some are designed especially for outside use. You may want to try some of these as you read through. Remember: when you are doing mindful activities with a child, do join in with them wherever possible.

Breathing exercises

Most of these exercises work with children aged 2 plus. Some younger children may find them hard, but with practice they can (and do) manage.

Breathing exercises are very useful to learn. They work across the ages and can be turned to at any time. We all have times when our breathing becomes shallow, and we might feel panicky and worried, with quicker breathing. Breathing exercises can help with this. As an adult, you may have been taught 7/11 breathing, a technique often used when someone is having a panic attack (breathe in for a count of 7, out for a count of 11). The breathing exercises I outline below are similar to this, but they work with young children as well as with older children, teenagers and adults.

Bubble breathing

This is probably my favourite breathing activity. It is the one I use in most training courses, and regularly with children.

You will need

▶ pot of bubbles

Dip the bubble wand into the pot of bubbles, take a deep breath, then blow slowly through the wand. Watch the bubbles – notice your breathing as you are watching, and repeat as many times as you want.

Bubble breathing through a straw

This activity works particularly well with a highy agitated child.

You will need

▶ straw
▶ bowl or cup of water

Dip the straw into the water, take a deep breath, then blow through the straw. Notice the bubbles rising upwards.

Hot chocolate breathing

This is lovely to do outside in Forest School while sitting round a fire.

You will need

▶ cup of hot chocolate

Make a cup of hot chocolate. Breathe in, sniffing the warm mug of hot chocolate Then breathe out, blowing on your hot chocolate to cool it down.

Feather breathing

You will need

▶ several feathers

Get the child to hold out their palm. Put the feather on their hand. Get them to take a deep breath and then gently blow out on to the feather. Watch the feather fly!

Flower breathing

This is particularly good if you use a dandelion.

You will need

▶ flower

Get the child to hold the flower out in front of them. Ask them to take a deep breath and sniff, and hold it for a count of 3, then to blow out through their mouth for a count of 3. If you are using a dandelion, watch the seeds fly.

Bee breathing

You will need

▶ the child to put their hands over their ears

Get the child to take a deep breath through their nose. Then, with their mouth closed, ask them to make a buzzing/humming noise as they breathe out through their nose.

Windmill breathing

You will need

▶ child's windmill (one with sails on a stick)

Get the child to hold the windmill in front of them and take a deep breath. The child then blows on to the sails and watches them move.

Rocking toy on tummy

You will need

▶ toy to go on the child's tummy

Get the child to lie on their back. Place the toy on their tummy. Tell the child they are going to rock the toy to sleep with their breathing. They need to breathe in deeply from their tummy, and then out. As they do this, their tummy will move and send the toy to sleep.

Finger breathing

You will need

▶ a hand!

Ask the child to hold their hand up in the air. Then inhale as they trace up the thumb, then exhale as you trace down the thumb. Proceed to inhale, tracing up the next finger, exhale down, etc. until you have traced all five of the child's fingers.

Rolling

You will need

▶ child to lie on their back
▶ mat or blanket (for comfort)

The child needs to hug their knees to their chest and close their eyes. Then get them to rock sideways a few times, taking deep breaths as they do this. They then roll forwards and backwards a few times, taking deep breaths in and out as they do. Afterwards, the child stretches out their legs and rests on the floor.

Finger fiddle

You will need

▶ child to sit, fingertips of both hands pressing together

Ask the child to take three deep breaths. They need to keep their fingertips together and tap their thumbs together three times, perhaps saying, 'Tap, tap, tap.' They repeat this with each of the other fingers. When they have to wriggle their fingers, they then shake their hands. Repeat this a few times.

Sea anemones

You will need

▶ child to lie on their back
▶ mat or blanket (for comfort)

Get the child to close their eyes and take a few deep breaths. Ask them to imagine that they are a sea anemone in the sea (you might need to show them a picture of a sea anemone), and their arms and legs the tentacles. Get them to wibble and wobble their arms and legs, pretending they are bobbing in the sea water.

Mindful eating

You will need

▶ small piece of fruit (for example, raisin, berry, small cracker)

Give the child the piece of food and get them to hold it in their palm. Explain that they will be eating it in a moment, but first they are going to notice it. Get them to look at it, observe how it looks and feels. Then ask them to smell it, and to take note how their mouth reacts when they do that. Next, they put in their mouth and hold it there, without eating it, noticing how that makes them feel. Then they can eat it. How did this make them feel? What did they notice?

Shake it about

You will need

▶ child to stand up straight

Get the child to take a few deep breaths in and out. Then ask them to hold their hands in the air and start shaking their arms – high in the air and low towards the ground. Next, the child starts shaking each leg, to the left and then to the right. They might want to shake their arms and legs at the same time, and give their whole body a good old shake. This might make them laugh and giggle. Then they can flop down on their back, take a deep sigh and stop.

Barefoot walking

You will need

▶ safe space to walk (if possible, one with different textures)

This is an incredible activity to do in all weathers, if it is snowing (dont do it for too long!). Get the child to take their shoes and socks off, and to walk, slowly. Ask them to note how it feels under their feet, and how it makes their body feel.

Sit and notice

You will need

▶ somewhere to sit (outside if possible)

Find a spot where the child can sit. See if they can:

▶ notice five things they can see
▶ find five things they can hear
▶ take note of they feel
▶ be aware of what they can smell.

Cloud watching

You will need

▶ a cloudy sky

Get the child to lie on their back and watch the clouds. Ask them to observe how they are moving, and to look at the shapes they make. Let them lie – and watch – and enjoy!

Explore something natural

You will need

▶ item from natural world (for example, feather, shell, flower, something the child has found)

Get the child to sit and hold the piece of nature they have found. Ask them to notice how it looks/feels. Does it smell? Does it make a sound?

Stand in the rain

You will need

▶ rainy day

Get the child to stand in the rain, and to notice the sound it makes. The child then puts their arms out and feels the drops of rain on their hands. Ask them to stick their tongue out and taste the rain. They can put their head back and let the rain drip on to their face. Ask them to think about how this feels.

Hug a tree

You will need

▶ tree

Get the child to stand close to a tree, and to notice the bark. How does it feel? They could touch it, or maybe put their face next to it. Ask them to see if they can put their hands around the tree. If it is a big tree, you might need to join hands with them and see if together you can hug it. You may need others to join you. Stand there for a few moments hugging the tree, taking on board how it feels.

Climb a tree

You will need

▶ tree with low branches

Enable the child to climb a tree. You may need to support them. This is not about you lifting them into the tree, but enabling them to climb one if they want to. When they are in the tree, encourage them to notice how it feels, looks, smells and sounds. How do they feel inside their body?

TAKE A MOMENT

There are a variety of ideas here. If any of them are new to you, spend some time considering which ones seem attractive to you. If there is something here you have not tried something before, try it out first on your own (or as a team) before using it with children.

Conclusion

With all of the ideas in this chapter, it is about finding ways to help children connect, notice and be curious about what is happening in their bodies. When we do mindful activities with children, we need to talk to them about the noticing, the slowing down and how they feel when they look at a flower, etc. We can talk to children openly from a young age about what we notice. For example, 'Poppy, I have noticed you are looking very calm and peaceful when you are sitting in a tree. How does it make you feel?' Hopefully this chapter has provided you with some mindful ideas to try and embed in your practice. These will support all children, but especially those who have experienced difficulties in their life.

Further information and references

Davy, A. (2019) *A Sense of Place: Mindful Practice Outdoors*. London: Featherstone/Bloomsbury.

Guber, T. and Kalish, L. (2005) *Yoga Pretzels: 50 Fun Yoga Activities for Kids & Grownups* [yoga cards]. Concord, MA: Barefoot Books.

Kinder, W. (2019) *Calm Mindfulness for Kids*. London: Dorling Kindersley.

Mindfulness in Schools Project (MiSP) (2021). Available at https://mindfulness inschools.org/about/

Oxford MYRIAD Project (2008–2021) MYRIAD: My Resilience in Adolescence. Available at http://myriadproject.org

Stewart, W. and Braun, M. (2017) *Mindful Kids: 50 Mindfulness Activities for Kindness, Focus and Calm* [deck of cards]. Concord, MA: Barefoot Books.

11 | Working with parents

The children we work with arrive in a package – with parents or carers. In this chapter I use the word 'parent' to incorporate anyone who cares for the child in the home. We know that parents are hugely influential on the children we work with and, sadly, we also know that this is not always a positive influence. Whatever our views on the way parents live their lives, and the decisions they make around parenting, we need to be able to engage and (where possible) work in partnership with them. PACEY share some useful ideas on how we can do this (see 'Further information and references').

Trust

For me, the key word here is 'trust'. We need the parents to trust that we will care for, protect, enrich and educate their child. We need them to have confidence that we will love and nurture their child. For some parents, this trust of another person can be so hard and, let's be honest, why should they have faith in us? What do they know about us? Just because we have a professional title, why should that mean we are trustworthy? For some of the families, trusting others in authority is such a huge ask of them: they may have had previous negative experiences of people in authority; they may be fearful about telling us things or what power we may have.

When I meet parents for the first time in the nurture outreach role, I try incredibly hard to let them know that I will be caring and protective of their child. I share with them ways I will be supporting their child's emotional development through sensory play and storytelling and the words I use with the child. Words are crucial. The emotion language I use with a child is carefully considered, but I am also careful in the words I use with parents. I make sure I am not using jargon and that I am inclusive in my language. In conjunction with this, I am careful about the tone of voice I use, the way I sit alongside them, the way I listen to their story, ensuring I am not just telling them what I am going to be doing with their child but that I am also hearing from them, learning from them about their child. For many of the parents I work with, they are fearful about how their child will be when they enter school, how they will behave. Some are worried the child will get excluded. There are worries about whether the child will make friends, if people will like them or if the child will manage full-time. It's important that we hear and listen to these worries and understand where they are coming from.

Not judging

I am highly aware that in society today it feels easy to judge others. We see it all the time on social media: we can look or hear about how others are behaving and jump to instant conclusions or judgements. We know this is unhelpful and often unkind, yet it can be so easy to fall into this habit. In our Early Years workplaces and schools, there can occasionally be a culture of judging parents. Sometimes I hear staff commenting on a parent's choice about the shoes they have bought their child, the food they give them, the way they spend their money, the decisions they have made. This is often not helpful. We need to stop and reflect once in a while and think for a moment about what we are seeing. Maybe we should ask a few more questions before we make a decision. I remember working with one social worker, a very experienced and wise woman. She told me that, every time she worked with a family, especially women who stayed in domestic violence situations, she would always remind herself that this could have been her experience if her life had gone a different way. Speaking for myself, I grew up with several ACEs. My life could have taken a very different route and, if I look back on one of my early relationship, I could easily have ended up in a very toxic place. Sometimes it is important to remember these things and to be compassionate.

In our role as Early Years educators, we must develop empathy, to help us to begin to understand what might be going on for a family. With children, we talk about the need to see the world through their eyes; to listen to them so we can begin to understand how life is for them. This is the same with parents. We must try to take a moment to see and understand how their life has been, and is now. We need curiosity and a wondering approach. This does not mean that we accept everything we see – when we see things are wrong, we need to speak out – but do this without being judgemental.

In one family I worked with, the child was showing extreme signs of being distressed. Mum was a drug addict and believed that her ability to parent was improved by taking cocaine. At first, I was so angry with her. I felt really judgemental about what she was doing in her parenting and the decisions she was making. I knew I was being judgemental, and I didn't feel comfortable about it. After talking it through in supervision, I had a conversation with the mother and I heard about her upbringing, how her dad had been a drug dealer and that her life had been chaotic. I then realised that she didn't know anything different, and the choices she was making came out of the experiences she herself had had as a child. That didn't mean that I agreed with her choices or supported her decisions. The other professionals and I still challenged her and offered support to help her make changes, but hearing her story helped me to be more compassionate and empathetic.

In my role of supporting children with additional social, emotional and mental health (SEMH) needs, I am aware it is all too easy to presume and judge without knowing what the full story is. In the same way we need to adopt a sense of curiosity with children, I believe we also need to adopt one with a family. Using the 'I wonder' phrase is so useful. For example, instead of judging about bedtime routine or food being offered, we could instead ask ourselves, 'I wonder why bedtimes are so tricky. What is it that makes this hard?' Or, instead of constantly remarking negatively on the food being offered in their child's lunchbox, asking a wondering question about why they are making the food choices: 'Is money tight? Or do they find it hard to say no if the child keeps asking for sweets, etc.?' This is something we can adopt within our supervision and team meeting practice, encouraging us all to maintain a curiosity and wondering culture instead of a judgemental one.

Previous experience in education

I have found that many parents I work with have had a negative experience of school themselves. They may have left education early, they may have experienced many different education settings, they may have found themselves in lots of trouble at school or just found it very difficult to achieve in school. When your own education story is negative, this can impact on how you feel about your own child entering school. I know, for myself, that I hated senior school, for a whole variety of reasons. Therefore, when my daughters reached that age, I needed to work hard not to put my issues and worries on to them or their school.

Some families carry the baggage and burden of their own education and put this on to their child's school, expecting that they and their child will 'be in trouble'. Education workers need to be mindful that not everyone has a positive view or experience of the world of education.

Building a relationship with parents early on is important. The children must know the adults who look after them are a team, and working together and saying the same things. This can only happen if we put the time into building relationships. This can take time, but it is worth it. Some staff in schools and nurseries have told me they don't have the time to spend it getting to know parents. In my experience, we often don't need to spend a lot of time with most parents to build a relationship, yet the time we do spend is always well spent. If we can build a relationship with parents where they realise they can trust us, this can go a long way in supporting the child, understanding the family and being able to support the family.

In another family I worked with, the child lived with his dad, who was very anxious about his son starting school. His own experience in school was very negative and Dad suffered from high anxiety. The school set up extra dates for him and the child to visit, on their own, and they had three additional visits on top of the usual transition dates. Once the child had started school, a member of school staff who has responsibility for supporting families met with Dad weekly to check in and make sure everything was OK. These extra support measures helped the child to settle and the dad to feel less anxious about school.

Partnership working

If we aim to work in partnership with parents, we need to look at the variety of ways we communicate with them, how we let them know about our setting and the work we do with the children, and also what we hope parents will be able to do. Often education language can feel like jargon to many parents. As Early Years educators we all understand the terms 'baseline data', 'phonics' and 'EYFS', but why would parents automatically know them? It is so important we think carefully about the words we use, how we explain to parents about the way we work with their children and also if there are key things we would like parents to do – for example, help their child to be able to put on their own coat, or support the child in being toilet trained, teach the child how to use a knife and fork or help the child to be able to wait for a moment. We know in the Early Years that it is so useful if a child can reach key developments such as these before they start school. However, parents may not realise this. As Early Years settings, we need to be clear and share information about how they can help their child in some of these developmental milestones, offering ideas on how they can do this. We must recognise that, if we are working in partnership with the parents, we sometimes need to assist them by sharing our experiences and ideas. There are many different ways we can do that. It might be through having leaflets, lending books on child development or having parents and staff evenings to talk about different developmental stages and how parents can help their child's development.

Pen Green, a children's centre based in Corby, in the United Kingdom, has a very good reputation for their outstanding work with parents. Throughout their work they have embedded the idea of working in partnership with parents. They are led by Margy Whalley, who has written an excellent book (2017) on the subject. Pen Green has set up a learning community where parents, practitioners and children all learn together. I remember hearing Margy speak at a conference, describing the way parents were being taught about schemas and were working on action research projects alongside staff about their children's schematic behaviours. This was inspiring and such a different way of working with parents, and I would suggest this is still an unusual practice. I am not aware of this kind of practice and encouragement happening in my area with parents and families currently. In my own role and team, we don't currently have the capacity to work with parents in this way, but I think it would hugely benefit our work if we did. If this is an area you would like to explore more, I highly recommend you look at the work at Pen Green (2021) and read Margy's book (2017).

TAKE A MOMENT

It is worth reviewing as a team how you work with parents. You might want to do a parent questionnaire to find out if there are key things they would like to find out. Ask the staff team how confident they are about working with parents. Is this an area where your team would benefit from professional development?

Being able to ask difficult questions

There are times when we need to ask parents some difficult questions, maybe around child protection concerns or developmental concerns. This is never easy, and I don't think it gets any easier with experience, but it is something we need to have the confidence to do. I have found the 'I wonder' phrase to be useful here. I have mentioned the phrase several times in the book where I use it with children, but I also find it useful when talking with parents. The phrase enables you to be curious, but not judgemental. For example, if I noticed Poppy has a bruise on her ear, I might ask, 'I was wondering what happened?' instead of 'How did Poppy get the bruise on her ear?' And 'I wonder what bedtime is like at home. How do you all experience it?' sounds less judgemental than 'Do you have a bedtime routine?' Similarly, 'I was wondering what you have found helps when Marley becomes very upset?' can bring some more discussion, instead of 'Marley is constantly having tantrums. What do you do at home when this happens?'

We need to be able to ask difficult questions and not shy away from them. I have noticed a lot of Early Years and education professionals can be afraid to ask questions around the area of mental health, and the same goes for domestic violence. Sometimes we need to say to a parent, 'I am wondering if you are safe in the house?' or 'I am wondering how your mental health is today? I know we have talked before about difficult days. Is today a difficult day?' For some, this can feel intrusive or outside of our remit. We are not mental health professionals or experts, but if we have built a trusting relationship with the parents we work with, where they know that their children's and their wellbeing is important to us, this makes it easier for us to ask questions and show concern. To be able to do this, we need good supervision practice, where we can go for support and share our concerns. We also need to know where we can signpost families who need additional support.

Signposting

If we have a relationship with families where parents feel able to be honest, and tell us what is happening, then we also need to be able to signpost to other agencies. As mentioned above, the majority of us are not mental health professionals. We are not experts in domestic violence or SEND support, and we don't need to be, as that is not our job, that is someone else's. However, we do have a responsibility to know about the local services in our area or, if we don't, someone in our team should.

The box itemises some of the agencies it is worth listing in your workplace. Too often, I have heard settings say they don't need this information, as the health visitor or school nurse has it. Health visitors and school nurses do have a wonderful array of information at their disposal, and we need to have good links with them, but it is far better to be able to pass on the relevant information at that moment rather than saying to a parent, 'I just need to find that out from the health visitor', as it could be several days or longer before you are able to get them the information. If you are signposting a family to another service, it is good practice to inform their health visitor (with the family's permission) if it is an Early Years child.

TAKE A MOMENT

Below is a list of some of the agencies it can be useful to have information about. Take a look and check if you do have details of these agencies in your setting. If you do not, task your team to get this information.

- ▶ local domestic violence support group (a charity, local authority or both
- ▶ local Citizens Advice service
- ▶ local family support charity or local authority team
- ▶ local SEND team (support for parents regarding SEND concerns)
- ▶ early help/intervention team (was the Common Assessment Framework/ CAF)
- ▶ local drug and alcohol service
- ▶ local (or national) bereavement charities
- ▶ local Mind branch
- ▶ number for Samaritans

Children's centres have this information to hand (they are excellent at sign-posting families to other organisations), but sadly in the UK there are not as many children's centres and very few now work with all families. This is even more of a reason for Early Years settings and schools to be well informed about their local services.

Interview with Ed Harker

In this part of the chapter, I interview Ed Harker, from our team. Before he started work with us, he was the teacher of a nursery class based in one of our local infant schools, the head teacher of the infant school. Below, he shares some of the ways he has worked with parents.

How can we work with parents? What are your top tips?

The first question I think we need to think about is if the setting is welcoming. Is there a parent room? Parent-friendly leaflets? Is it first names you are using? How do you talk to the parents?

Using first names is really interesting, as your approach has always been first name. I remember when you were a headteacher, everyone knew you as Ed. What was your thinking there?

There is something boundary-reducing about it and it can be disarming. Most people have deep emotional memories of teachers and headteachers, and not all of those are good. Anything which reinforces that, like 'Mr So-and-So', we don't often use that language in our daily life. We usually refer to people's names. It can be echoes of schooling, which is not always a happy memory, so breaking that is helpful. It was useful for me as a bloke as it deformalises things.

What do you mean by the 'parent room'?

A parent room, if you have the facility and space – but most places don't have space – it's an area where you can sit away from the hubbub. Often it is near the cloakroom. Or have it set up in the outdoor space, just outside the front door of the setting. Have a bench, somewhere that you can have nice quiet conversations, where you are not calling parents into an office. It's slightly separate, it's a designated grown-up space – for example, it has seating at normal height. When I was a headteacher, we put benches in the playground. I was keen to create a community environment for the parents not just a learning environment for the children. We created conversation spaces with the way we placed the benches around the playground.

That's about the welcome. How do you then start to build relationships with parents?

Encourage people to have a look around on busy days, but also being flexible so they can visit when the place is empty, as some people are really nervous, and when it is empty that might be easier. Then the next key thing is home visits. It shows a demonstration of mutuality and trust. It's a symbolic act to be invited into somebody's home. For many families, the only people who visit their home in an official capacity are social workers – maybe police and health workers. As educators, you are a benign official group who can come in. It meant the child associated you with home, which is usually good. We always did the visits in pairs: one practitioner would be with the grown-up, and one practitioner with the child. And the child often says, 'Come and see my bedroom.' The practitioner will check this is OK with the parent, and then you go up and see their room and notice what their quilt cover is – Buzz Lightyear or Frozen. You can then connect that with the child when they are back in school. Also, while they are upstairs playing and seeing the bedroom, the other practitioner can ask the more tricky questions to the parent. So you are building a relationship with the child and adult.

Home visits are also a good way of capturing the emotional atmosphere of a family, which can be a really hard thing to pick up. Some families are materially very advantaged but emotionally disadvantaged; that was a real eye-opener for me. I noticed home visits could challenge prejudices and preconceptions: to be going into what felt like a rough area or maybe one with limited opportunities, but often those children had a very loving family, with extended family and many people around them. In comparison, you could go into other places that felt very uptight, very clean and lots of stuff, and it didn't feel at ease or loving. Also, you can start to have conversations. People talk about things in their own home that they won't talk about anywhere else. People point things out: 'That's granny' or 'That's the cat.' 'We have damp in the room' or 'We don't have a garden.' You often have a more natural conversation with people in their own homes.

Do you think, as an educator, the home visit helps you to have a fuller idea about the child and what their daily lived experience is?

Yes, you develop a more rounded picture of the child and their strengths and development needs. Also, you might know what book or toy is their favourite. The other side is, you might have a sense that they are quite secure, so might be able to let them cry for a little bit. Or, if Mum says, 'No I am going', and just walks, you know a little bit more and know if that is OK. Or you might think, 'No, that isn't right', and suggest she stays for another five minutes. You can nuance it a bit more, as you have more knowledge. They are also good, because as a team you can understand the community more. You have professional conversations afterward about what you saw and heard and what is happening in the community you are serving. Also, by walking to the visits, you get to know the route the children take to school. Often staff drive into work and then drive away at the end of the day. They don't necessarily know all the local streets, footpaths, trees and parks. By walking to the visits, you are getting a fuller idea of the community.

There are always some families who don't want to engage. Maybe their experience of school was negative, or maybe there are so many other professionals involved, it feels too much. What are your tips around this?

Some families need you to be persistent. The difficulty we had was when some children came from a previous setting where they were too scared to mention things to the parents. I understand why, as some of the parents could appear intimidating, but somebody had to be able to go up to them and have those trickier conversations. That is what is good about the home visits, as you have already had some of those jollier conversations. Pick your moment, start with all the positive news. If there are issues, start building with happy things. Also, we used speculative language – for example, 'We have noticed that …' or 'Have you ever noticed that …?' It's also talking about the behaviour instead of the child. We used the 'I notice' phrase as a team quite a lot, as it depersonalises it. We might say, 'As a team we have noticed that Jonny is fascinated in the sinks. Does he do that at home?' or 'We have noticed he loves throwing things. Does he do that in the park?' Grandparents can be useful, too, as grandparents often notice things, if they are doing the drop-off or pick-up. Sometimes they are happy to share their thoughts or engage in conversations.

We need to be careful that we are not patronising families. It is quite tricky in how we do that, but we need to recognise that they know their child so well, and we are looking forward to finding out more about their child. Saying it in an honest and not a patronising way is a skill. In the early days of the child being in the setting, aim to discover something or capture a picture of the child doing something and feed that back to the parent. Every parent wants to know that their child is valued, is a special individual.

My last thought: I was a big fan of newsletters. I would take digital photos of children, and put together the photos and a few headlines with a picture on the back of a child's drawing, and photocopy them for all parents. Digital copies just vanish, but a paper copy is around. Children look at them, parents look at them. It's a basic and simple way to share the lovely things we have been doing. It draws people in and helps them to feel part of the nursery or school community.

Views from parents

To end this chapter, I spoke with a group of parents, asking them what they would like to know about education settings to help them in settling their child. These are some of their answers:

- a conversation about separation for the child and parent, and some tips on how we could support the child at home

- advice and ideas on routines at home that would support the start in nursery/school

- advice around what to do when your child does not want to go to school/nursery and the separation anxiety for the child

- tell us there will be meltdowns from the child at the end of the day at home; that this is normal and it is linked to the child being exhausted by all they have been doing in the day

- remind us that school is different, even if the child has been in nursery full time – the experience at school is different and children can be exhausted for most of the first term, sometimes most of the first year.

- some ideas on how to talk to our child at the end of the day about their day, without bombarding them with questions

- advice around how to create a space for children to tell us if something is wrong or they are worried

- let us know it is normal to feel lonely and sad when your child starts school

- if the setting could write up a line or two about what they have done that day, I can then talk to my child about it

- regular newsletters would help us to know a bit more about what is happening – it all feels so alien and I don't know what they do

- when staff know my child's name and their interest and show me they care for and love my child, that makes a huge difference – I feel like I can trust them when I see that

- I want to know it is OK to tell you if my child is finding it hard or has fallen out with a child, or they are worried; I want to know you will listen to me and my child.

I find these comments really interesting. They remind me that the transition to nursery or school is as huge for parents as it is for children. I know many schools and nurseries do a parents' information session or parents' evening to share information. However, what stood out for me most in these comments is a sense of the parents wanting some guidance on how they can support their child. Not so much the formalities, or school uniform, or timings, or what they do in nursery or school, but more about advice and information on what they can do if their child finds it hard to settle or practical ideas about how to manage the end of the day when the child is exhausted. I know some teachers do not feel this is their job – that this is more parenting advice – but I feel that it is our job, as Early Years educators, to be able to offer some thoughts or suggestions. Maybe the nursery could think about this and offer some thoughts before the child leaves nursery. Perhaps the Early Years setting and school together could create a leaflet giving a few top tips, such as ideas for a routine when a child gets home (as they will be so tired) or strategies to support the child if they don't want to leave you in the morning.

Conclusion

If we can build a trusting relationship with parents, this will hugely benefit the child, parents and setting. Although this sometimes involves more time and effort, the benefits far outweigh any potential negatives or time issues. It is worth spending time as a team thinking about how we work with parents, considering changes that could be made. Discover from parents what they would have found useful when their child first started at your setting – what support they wanted or what types of information they may have found helpful. It may also be worth finding out from parents how the setting should communicate with them. We sometimes roll out the same parent meetings or leaflets and/or display boards without asking if this works for the current cohort of parents. We need to tweak and adapt the way we work with different cohorts of children, and the same applies to the way we work together with their parents.

 Further information

PACEY (Professional Association for Childcare and Early Years) (2009–2021) Spotlight on … Working in Partnership with Parents Available at www.p acey.org.uk/working-in-childcare/spotlight-on/partnerships-with-parents/
Pen Green Centre for Children and Their Families (2021) Avaialble at www .pengreen.org
Whalley, M. (2017) *Involving Parents in Their Children's Learning: A Knowledge Sharing Approach.* London: SAGE Publishing.

12 | Wellbeing of adults

The subject of wellbeing has become increasingly popular. When I first wrote my books on the wellbeing of staff and children (Mainstone-Cotton 2017a, 2017b), it was only just being talked about, and there were limited books on the subject. We now live in a time where there is a greater understanding of wellbeing, and it is being addressed by an increasing number of people across various sectors. I think it's a really positive move forward: policies are being written on the topic and we are giving it more attention. However, when it has so much attention – particularly when celebrities talk and write about it so much – there is a danger that it gets viewed as frivolous, luxury or a mere fad.

This chapter explores how we need to look after our own wellbeing, so that we can then look after the wellbeing of the children we work with. It is important for everybody. It's not a luxury and it's not a frivolous act, and it is essential for people who work with children who have social, emotional and mental health (SEMH) needs. The stories that we hear of children's lives, sometimes the behaviours we encounter, can be incredibly stressful.

Louise Bombèr (2007) talks about how we can take on secondary stress – the stress we take on of others – and I think this is particularly relevant in our work with children with SEMH needs. At the end of the day or week, when we are feeling strained, it can help to ask, 'Is this my stress or the stress of another person?' In this chapter, I share ideas and current research around wellbeing. This research has developed so much over the last few years and I mention some of the new findings. I will also share some stories: how I have learned to really pay attention to my wellbeing, what that looks like in practice and how I support my co-workers in paying attention to their wellbeing.

Stress

Whenever we talk about wellbeing, we need to address stress, as that's probably one of the main things that has a huge impact on our wellbeing. We all experience stress, and it isn't necessarily a bad thing. We need it in our lives to get up in the morning, to go to work and to have some motivation to get on. The difficulty arises when stress takes over or when it begins to impact our physical and mental health and our relationships. The problem is, we all experience stress in different ways and what one person can find incredibly stressful, another person may find motivating. We all need to figure out what our own relationship is with stress and to learn the triggers and warning signs in our own bodies. It's going to be different for all of us. In the United Kingdom, I don't think we are very good at talking about how we recognise stress in our bodies or minds.

We talk a lot about stress. It has often become a buzzword – we just say the word without even thinking about it. But I wonder how many of us really know how our bodies tell us when we are overly stressed? We need to be able to identify how our bodies tell us when we are stressed. This varies for everybody. For me, the warning signs in my body are when my jaw tightens, my breathing becomes shallow and my shoulders and neck hurt, causing headaches and sometimes migraines. Once we recognise that our body is telling us we are stressed, we can be proactive and put things into place to help ourselves.

Many years ago, when my younger daughter was a baby, I returned to work. My job was quite challenging, and juggling a toddler, a baby and a stressful job wasn't going very well for me. The stress increased and I didn't know how to identify that or how to manage it. I felt under pressure from my boss and I constantly felt like I wasn't good enough. I wasn't getting it right either for my children or in my job. It reached a crisis point when I had excruciating pain in my head, so I went to see my GP and he immediately sent me to the hospital, as he thought I had a brain tumour. After various scans and tests, it turned out to be stress-related. When the headaches stopped and I returned to work, I remember driving to work and deciding I was never going to allow the stress of work make me ill again. For the short time I was in the hospital, I remember clearly thinking my babies needed me and nothing was worth getting in the way of that.

How stress works in the body

Many different things act as stressors to us. This could be work, family, expectations, discrimination, money, plus many others. Our bodies can see these as threats or potential threats, and stress is what happens in our minds and bodies when we encounter one of these threats. In earlier chapters, I wrote about the way children can go into the stress response of fight/flight/freeze, and the same goes for adults. The stressor may be different, but it's the same response. Our heart beats faster, our muscles tense, our digestion slows down and our immune function changes. When we are flooded with the stress response we start to feel it in our body and our mind; we can become ill or find it hard to concentrate and make decisions. This can have long-term consequences on our health if our body is continually dealing with stress.

After I had recovered from being ill, it was the first time I began to understand that stress can have serious consequences, and I didn't want that to happen again. Looking back now, I didn't really understand about stress and wellbeing, and what I could do to support and take care of myself. The one thing I knew did help me was being in my garden. I did a little bit of gardening back then – there wasn't much time with two young children in my life. But I realised just being in the garden and being outside helped me. I'm now in a very different place, 20 years on, with regards to wellbeing and stress. I've learned through experience and reading just how important it is to find the things that help us. My garden is still a place of sanctuary for me, the place where I can go and immediately nourish myself through being outside. By spending an hour weeding, digging and planting, I can totally switch off from everything else going on. For me, gardening has become a mindful act and an essential tool in my wellbeing toolbox. Throughout this chapter, I am going to share ideas about what can be in your wellbeing toolbox.

TAKE A MOMENT

Take a moment to think about are the stress warning signs in your body. Where does it show up in your body? Your answer might be similar to the one you gave in the exercise in Chapter 10 (regarding how/when you know you need to relax). You may also respond differently.

When we have identified that stress is affecting us and we have identified what it is, then we need some strategies to help lower the stress. Sometimes we need to take radical action – we may need to make a big change in our life. Other times, we can make some tweaks, maybe having the courage to say no to something, or making some changes to what we eat or how we sleep (I discuss both of these later in the chapter). On occasion, it can feel that we are not able to prevent a particular stress – for example, if someone we love is ill or we are waiting for a difficult outcome. Whatever the stress, knowing the things that help our stress levels, and being more intentional about putting those into place, goes some way to supporting us. Often, when we are in the middle of a stressful situation it can be hard to problem-solve and think about what we can do. It can be helpful to come up with a list of ways that help you, and do this when you are feeling calm. Then you have it to refer to when you are struggling and might find it hard to remember. I have a photo board on my desktop page, on which I put photos of things that make me happy; the things that help me when I feel stressed and low. When I find it all too much, I open this page and remind myself about what helps me.

The top five things that help my stress levels

▶ swimming daily
▶ coldwater swimming
▶ gardening
▶ walking in nature
▶ being with and talking to friends and family

When stress leads to burnout

An extreme consequence of stress is when it leads to burnout. Working in education, I am aware that many teachers and heads end up burned out. To be honest, in these Covid-19 times, I am concerned that many more people in education may end up in a similar state. I recently heard a podcast of Brené Brown interviewing Emily and Amelia Nagoski (2020) (also see 'Further information and references'). Emily and Amelia are twins and (based both on their experiences and research) have been exploring the subject of stress, burnout and becoming stuck in our emotions. They link burnout to emotional exhaustion, and emotional exhaustion to becoming stuck in an emotion and a stress cycle. An example of this could be when we return to a stressful job every day. We may feel stuck in the feelings of rage, grief and despair if they are continuously part of our experience and we can't find a way through it. Emily and Amelia suggest that we all need to complete the stress response cycle, and we need to do this most days, as we experience stress most days. They describe the stress response cycle as a way of allowing our bodies to feel that it has survived the threat and that you are now safe. They suggest a few key ways that can help us to complete the stress cycle (Nagoski and Nagoski 2020):

▶ *Exercise*: Move your body, through dance, running, cycling, swimming, walking. Around 20 plus minutes a day should help.

► *Breathing*: Using deep slow breathing exercises. Breathe deeply so your belly moves. There is growing research to show that slow nasal breathing lowers blood pressure, reduces cortisol (stress hormone) and boosts your immune system (also see 'Further information and references'). The bee breathing in Chapter 10 is an example of nasal breathing.

► *Connecting with others*: Being with people and connecting with them, even if this is only chatting to the checkout person on the till while you are at the supermarket. In the current Covid-19 crisis, one huge stressor for people has been the lack of connecting with other people; connecting virtually does not feel the same.

► *Laughter*: Real laughter – the type of laughter that makes your belly hurt.

► *Physical affection*: The idea of a six-second kiss and a twenty-second hug. This is the time to help your body know you are safe. Interestingly it is thought that completing the cycle with affection can also be found through petting an animal, as this too can lower your blood pressure.

► *Crying*: A good cry can help. It, too, can help to complete the cycle. I know I sometimes choose to watch a very sad film, as I know that I will feel better once I have sobbed through it.

► *Creative engagement*: Writing poetry, drawing, making sculpture, playing an instrument. For centuries, we have seen how artists sort through their feelings and emotions, and their creative expression. This can help us to complete the stress cycle, as well.

TAKE A MOMENT

Earlier in the chapter, I asked you to take a moment to think about how stress shows itself in your body. I now invite you to take a moment to think about what helps you to complete the stress cycle. Are there ideas from the list that you could use?

Finding your thing

Whenever wellbeing is discussed, a few main topics usually get a mention (alongside stress): eating well, exercising, getting enough sleep, mindfulness and experiencing joy. For many of us, we know that having good routines and rhythms is crucial for our wellbeing. Vital steps that to support us include good practices such as eating well, lowering or cutting out alcohol consumption, exercising, getting enough sleep, practising mindfulness, and observing self-love and compassion. However, with so much information out there, it can be hard to know where to focus, who to listen to, where to go. We all need to find our thing. We have to discover the voices that we want to listen to, the exercise that will work for us, the food that we can eat and the daily rhythm that will enrich us. Here, I look briefly at some of these subjects and make links to people and research I have found helpful. I am not an expert in these areas, but I have read around and found others whom I trust and can learn from. You may have your own people, but just in case you don't, I share mine here.

Eating well

This is a growing area that many are now exploring and looking at, The link between our minds and bodies, and how food and drink can affect this connection, is increasingly recognised. I am aware there are many voices speaking about this subject, and sometimes it can be hard to know who to listen to: who is speaking from a scientific place, and who is (quite frankly) making some questionable links. There are many people out there doing podcasts, writing books and blogs that sell a whole host of different products about food and nutrition. If you feel overwhelmed and are struggling to find a way through, you are not alone – this area can feel very confusing.

Two GPs I have discovered in the last few years who have written books and have podcasts are Dr Rangan Chatterjee and Dr Rupy Aujla (Chatterjee 2018; Dr Chatterjee 2020; The Doctor's Kitchen 2021 in 'Further information and references'). I like the fact that they are both practising GPs, so they are coming from a medical and scientific base, and in their podcasts they interview many different experts. Dr Rupy has a specialist interest in food and how that can support us medically. He has had TV cooking shows, as well as written several cookbooks, plus a podcast. Dr Rangan specialises in stress and looks at ways to support ourselves when we are stressed, looking at diet, exercise and our mind. I have used both of their books a lot, but I particularly like Dr Chatterjee's (2018) The Stress Solution. I go back to this time and time again – so much so, I bought a copy for both my daughters!

Exercising

This is an area where it is particularly important to find your thing. For some people, the word 'exercise' leaves them feeling inadequate, fearful and may bring back bad memories from school. For others, it may be the thing that brings them the most joy. Until eight years ago, I would have put myself in the first category, I hated the idea of exercise – running gave me a headache, I have fallen off many bikes, I have dyspraxia – so any form of exercise that involves catching or throwing or generally being well coordinated was a no-go area for me. But I could tolerate swimming, so I decided I needed to sort out this fitness thing in my own life, and I took up swimming five days a week at my local pool, in the early morning slot. It took around two months to begin to get used to it, and by six months I realised I loved it. Eight years on, though, and I am totally hooked. Lockdown felt physically and mentally painful when I couldn't swim every day. I missed it so badly. (If I am honest, I missed it a lot more than seeing people.) As I write this, I am now back in the pool at 6.30 a.m. every Monday to Friday for my 30-minute slot. I have just finished the eighth week of being back, and I can't express how grateful I am for being able to swim every weekday again. Those 30 minutes are my time, when I am not just exercising but it's when I can process what is in my head – or I can totally switch off. I can enter the pool feeling down and leave it 30 minutes later feeling calm and peaceful.

Three years ago, I started to discover the joy of outdoor swimming. I realised I enjoyed the coldwater experience. This is partially linked with experiencing peri-menopause, because suddenly the cold water was no longer a horrific idea! Over the last few years, I have totally embraced coldwater swimming. If I lived by the beach, I would swim daily, all year round in the sea. But I don't live near the coast, so instead I river-swim, pond-swim and travel to the coast when I can. I try to coldwater swim at least two or three times a month – often more. Thankfully, I have persuaded my husband that coldwater swimming is a good thing and we now book holidays and day trips based around it. Last year, we swam all winter. I don't swim in a wetsuit, as that feels constricting. There is something about the cold water which leaves me feeling amazing and so alive and, although this sounds mad, the pain of the water in the winter is strangely releasing. If I am stressed, a coldwater swim immediately brings down my stress levels, to the extent where family and friends now ask me if I have a swim booked. Some fascinating research looks at how cold water is thought to help stress and anxiety (see 'Further information' at the end of the chapter). As I said, the key is finding your thing, what works for you. I do realise, for many of you reading this, that the coldwater swimming idea sounds crazy, and I'm not suggesting this is the one thing that will work for you. For others, it will be running, or fell walking, or trampolining, or roller skating, or dancing or boxing. It doesn't matter what it is, but finding some exercise that brings you joy will enhance your life.

Sleep

Scientists are now beginning to gain a greater understanding of the importance of sleep and how being sleep deprived can have serious consequences on our mental and physical health. However, even though there is growing evidence to suggest how critical sleep is, it's still not widely talked about. For many people, struggling to go to sleep or staying asleep are signs they are stressed. The recommended amount of sleep for adults is around seven to nine hours' sleep a night. Matthew Walker (2017), a neuroscientist specialising in sleep, suggests that two-thirds of adults in the developed world fail to get their recommended amount, and many don't realise this is a problem. Before you continue reading, take a moment to think how much sleep you get most nights.

There is worrying evidence to show a link between lack of sleep and lowered immunity and double the risk of cancer, and an ongoing lack of sleep has been linked with the onset of Alzheimer's. Not only is sleep vital for physical health, but it also supports our ability to learn, problem-solve and make decisions. For most of us, we can think of times when we know lack of sleep has impacted our ability to think and make decisions. I know that I am dreadful if I do not get enough sleep. I become very grumpy, I find it hard to be clear-headed and I also find the usual easiest of jobs a huge challenge. Some describe the trinity of wellbeing – diet, exercise and sleep – suggesting that these three areas are all vital for our mental and physical wellbeing.

Within the area of sleep, there is a phrase 'good sleep hygiene' – the things we can do to support ourselves to get enough sleep. This includes:

- Have a regular sleep schedule – go to bed and get up at the same time each day.
- Don't exercise before you go to bed – try to have a gap of two to three hours between exercise and bedtime.
- Avoid caffeine, nicotine and alcohol before bed.
- Avoid a large meal before bed.
- Sleep in a cool room.
- Sleep in a dark room.
- Turn off devices for at least an hour before bed.
- Take a hot bath before you go to bed.
- Have a hot drink before bed.
- Don't lie in bed struggling to sleep. If, after 20 minutes, you find you have not fallen asleep, get up and do something relaxing until you feel sleepy.

Mindfulness

Mindfulness is an area that has grown hugely recently, as has the number of people practising it. In Chapter 10, I wrote about using the practice with children, and how we need to model this, as well as use it ourselves (so allowing us to successfully support children in the practice). Mindfulness is linked with breathing and meditation practice. In my experience, you need to work at it, as it doesn't always come easily or naturally. When I first heard about mindfulness, I was under the impression it is all about sitting still, emptying your mind and finding calmness, but this was a misunderstanding (and I suspect many others have it, too). Mindfulness helps us to be present, to be aware of what is going in the moment. It enables greater self-awareness and can help us to lower stress and find some calmness.

If mindfulness is a new area to you, or you have practised this with children but not very much on your own, I recommend trying the eight-week mindfulness course with Mark Williams (see 'Further information and references'). Many mindfulness courses in the United Kingdom use his course, and you can also buy his book. Because this is a growing market, a variety of apps and books is available (again, see 'Further information and references'). If you find the idea of sitting and stopping too difficult (some people, who have experienced trauma, find mindfulness triggering for them), perhaps try yoga practice instead. It uses many mindfulness ideas, but also brings in movement and breathing. For some, the movement and breathing exercises together help them to move out of their mind and their too-active thoughts. I have practised mindfulness for about six years. I found it very helpful, but I still find that sometimes, when my brain is too active, sitting is still too hard. I have developed a nature walking mindful practice, which I have used for a while, but it became especially important and useful during lockdown. My daily sunrise walks through the community meadow and in the fields became a mindful walk for me. When I stood in the field and felt and watched the sunrise, my mind was able to slow down.

I also find barefoot walking a mindful activity. If you're new to mindfulness, I would encourage you to take five minutes away from reading this book and try a barefoot walk. Even if you are a mindfulness regular, do a barefoot walk anyway. (See 'Further information and references' for more information on mindfulness and yoga.)

1   Go outside to an area where it is safe to walk without shoes and socks on.
2   Take off your shoes and socks.

3   Walk, and notice how it feels under your feet.
4   Notice how this activity slows you down.
5   Notice how your body responds to this activity.

It is very hard to do barefoot walking quickly. It forces you to slow, to take notice, to be aware and in that moment. For me, barefoot walking is one of the mindful exercises I can do, along with coldwater swimming, that I know will always help me to feel calmer. Try it on different surfaces – grass, gravel, concrete, sand, mud (it is particularly amazing in the snow!) I love using barefoot walking in conferences and workshops I deliver with adults. It seems to invoke a level of surprise and often helps people to relax into the session. I also use it regularly with the children I support. It is such a simple exercise that you can use it anywhere. I recommend teachers and nursery workers, if they are feeling overwhelmed, to take a few minutes and do a barefoot mindful exercise. You could do this inside the setting, but for me it works even better outside.

Self-compassion

When you read or listen to books or podcasts on the subject of wellbeing, you don't always hear about self-compassion, but I believe it needs to be in the top five wellbeing areas. I first came across the term 'self-compassion' when reading Brené Brown and Kristin Neff (see 'Further information and references' for details on both). When I first read their ideas, it was a lightbulb moment for me. I grew up with a mum who has bipolar, and one trait I inherited was to self-criticise and to catastrophise. I didn't need anyone else to be critical of me – I had lots of self-criticisms – and would often play over words I said or relive events over and over in my head. Sadly, along with this, when I was experiencing something joyful, in the back of my head I would have the thought that it would soon change and something bad would happen. I thought this was just me, but reading Brené and Kristin helped me to understand what was going on in my head. I could stop this and learn to be kind to myself.

A crucial part of self-compassion and kindness comes through the words I use on myself and noticing when I am falling down a spiral of negativity. Kristin Neff (2011) talks about using a self-script. In Chapter 7, I wrote about using scripts with children and how useful they can be, so when I read her book (already familiar with the idea), it seemed natural to use a script for myself. I use a few scripts. When I am driving to a school and feeling low or a sense of dread about what

I may encounter, I say to myself, 'It's OK to be concerned, but you can do this, you have done it before and you will do it again.' The other words I use were inspired by Brené Brown. She often talks about the story you tell yourself. Is it the real story? I found this really helpful when I find myself catastrophising, so when I notice I am doing this, I will say to myself, 'Stop.' Sometimes I put my hand up and then ask myself, 'Is this the real story?' It has taken a lot of practice, but it has helped me so much.

Learning to be kind and compassionate to myself has helped me to be kinder and more compassionate to others. Over the years I have realised that being kind to myself is linked to eating well, getting enough sleep, exercising, wild swimming and mindfulness. These are all kindness acts and examples of self-compassion that don't necessarily impact others, but they hugely impact me. They are all linked with knowing myself well and finally realising what helps me to be well and stay well, and then to practise these, actively putting them into place so they are firmly part of my routine.

Experiencing joy

We all experience joy in many different ways. It is not something that our brain immediately holds on to, so we need to recognise it and embrace it for it to stay in our memory. When we are feeling stressed and hassled, it can be easy not to notice the joy in our lives. There have been many wellbeing and happiness studies across the world, which indicate that Scandinavian countries are often the most happy. One theory for this is the amount of time they spend outside. In Chapter 9, I wrote how important it is for children to be outside, and this also applies to adults. I recently discovered the word *friluftsliv*, a Norwegian word that translates as 'open-air living'. *Friluftsliv* is about embracing an outdoor lifestyle and the ways this can enhance happiness and bring joy (see Delorie 2020). Throughout this book, I have mentioned various activities that bring me joy, and I am aware they are all based outdoors – coldwater swimming, sunrise walks, looking for the owl family and gardening. I have just come back home from a few days in Cornwall, where I spent my time mostly walking the coast path and swimming in the sea. Each time I swam, I was so conscious of how good it felt to be alive. I experienced so much joy in this time. (See 'Further information and references' for more on coldwater swimming.)

Before moving on, think just for a moment about what brings joy to your life and how often you experience it.

How this links to supporting children with SEMH needs

Throughout this book, I have highlighted how working with children who have SEMH needs can sometimes be challenging, stressful and emotionally draining. The ability to do this is only possible if you take care of yourself, however. Children know when you are low or not working at your best, and children with SEMH needs often pick up on the smallest of changes in a person. They are often so hypervigilant, they will know when something is not right and this can cause increased anxiety for them. If you work with any children it is important to support your own wellbeing, but it is even more vital to do this if you work with children with SEMH needs. You need to have a range of tools that assist you. You also need to be highly self-aware, and in touch with what is going on in your body and with your emotions and feelings. For me, it is essential that you have colleagues who can support and back you.

Earlier in the chapter, I mentioned having our own wellbeing toolbox. This could be a box with ideas in or a list of ideas and/or pictures, which you can use as a reminder of what supports your wellbeing. As I mentioned earlier, when we are stressed we can easily forget the things that help us and we sometimes need a reminder. Below are some of the things that are in my wellbeing kit:

▶ *Hand cream*: I carry this in my bag and car. When things feel difficult, a small moment of self-care is to give myself a hand massage – taking five minutes to massage my hands gently, noticing how this helps me to feel more relaxed.
▶ *Swimming and coldwater swimming*: As mentioned earlier, I have photos on my laptop and phone to remind me how much joy this brings me.
▶ *People to speak to*: I have a list of five people on my phone, to remind me who I can turn to if I need support. This includes family, friends and colleagues.
▶ *Eating well*: I try to ensure that I always eat regularly, don't skip breakfast and eat lots of fruit and veg.
▶ *Being in nature*: I know that if I go into the garden or go for a walk, I will feel better.
▶ *Mindfulness*: I use the Buddhify app (see 'Further information and references') and outdoor walking, as mentioned above.
▶ *Hot bath*: I find this always helps me to find some calmness at the end of the day. I often use lavender essential oil in the bath, which also helps with calmness.
▶ *Sleepy tea*: There are various ones on the market, and this is part of my daily routine before I go to bed. The camomile and valerian in the tea are supposed to help with sleep.

► *Devices*: I have set myself a rule that I won't look at emails or social media after 7.00 p.m. This is particularly important to me on the days when I am working. I can easily become agitated by things I have read, and these can stay in my mind if I read them near bedtime.

► *Music and reading*: Both books and music can help me to switch off. Certain playlists and artists I listen to will help me feel calmer, and a good novel often helps me to switch off entirely.

As you finish reading this chapter, I would encourage you to take some time to create your own wellbeing toolkit. Think about what helps you, what nourishes you. You might want to keep this list in an easily accessible place, so you can be reminded of its contents.

Conclusion

With many celebrities writing about wellbeing, together with numerous products selling us wellbeing tools, it is easy to believe that we can only support our wellbeing if we have a lot of time and money. I hope this chapter has indicated a few ways we can all make small changes, there are things we can each do, that do not involve spending money or take lots of time. However, by making these small changes, they could help us and support our wellbeing.

 Further information and references

Bombèr, L. (2007) *Inside I'm Hurting: Practical Strategies for Supporting Children with Attachment Difficulties in School*. Duffield: Worth Publishing.
Brené Brown (2021) Available at https://brenebrown.com
Brené Brown (2020) Brené with Emily and Amelia Nagoski on Burnout and How to Complete the Stress Cycle. Available at https://brenebrown.com/podcast/brene-with-emily-and-amelia-nagoski-on-burnout-and-how-to-complete-the-stress-cycle/
Buddhify (2021) Meditation Done Differently. Available at https://buddhify.com
Chatterjee, R. (2018) *The Stress Solution: The 4 Steps to a Calmer, Happier, Healthier You*. London: Penguin.
Delorie, O. L. (2020) *The Nordic Art of Friluftsliv: Reconnect with Nature*. London: White Lion Publishing/Quarto.

The Doctor's Kitchen (2021) Available at https://thedoctorskitchen.com

Dr Chatterjee (2020) Feel Better. Live More. Available at https://drchatterjee
.com

Mainstone-Cotton, S. (2017a) *Promoting Emotional Wellbeing in Early Years Staff: A Practical Guide for Looking After Yourself and Your Colleagues.* London: Jessica Kingsley.

Mainstone-Cotton, S. (2017b) *Promoting Young Children's Emotional Health and Wellbeing: A Practical Guide for Professionals and Parents.* London. Jessica Kingsley.

Mindfulness Exercises (2021) Mark Williams on Mindfulness. Available at https://mindfulnessexercises.com/mark-williams-mindfulness/

Nagoski, E. and Nagoski, A. (2020) *Burnout: Solve Your Stress Cycle.* London: Penguin.

Neff, K. (2011) *Self Compassion.* London: HarperCollins.

Outdoor Swimming Society (2021) Cold Water as a Medical Treatment. Available at www.outdoorswimmingsociety.com/cold-water-therapy/

Self-Compassion (2021) Self-Compassion: Dr Kristin Neff. Available at https://self-compassion.org

Spotify (2020) Why Changing the Way You Breathe Will Transform Your Body andMind with James Nestor. Feel Better, Live More with Dr Rangan Chatterjee, Episode 124. Available at https://open.spotify.com/episode/20IoFY7dQC41C8SKbnhMln?si=V66_2veeRTOg_aFf28j_ug&fbclid=IwAR3Heye11j8jPsCCKNTDcQTFp_LM0zp4whjsVWCImMArh7-mtXoOeTKCZvQ

Walker, M. (2017) *Why We Sleep: The New Science of Sleep and Dreams.* London: Penguin.

Yoga with Adriene (2021) Available at https://yogawithadriene.com

Conclusion

I hope this book has offered you some insight into children with social, emotional and mental health (SEMH) needs. When I started writing it, I was aware that they can often easily fall under the label of being difficult, angry, impulsive. I know some adults are frightened of working with children who display these needs, or believe that they are intentionally difficult and naughty. I really hope that I have started to shine a light on what might be happening for these children and that I may have started to unpick and explore what may be occurring for them. I also trust that I have shown that not all children with SEMH needs express this through challenging behaviour. As we know, every child is different. Maybe I have helped you to see how the world is sometimes viewed through children's eyes. But most of all I hope I have helped you to see there are many tweaks and changes that we can all make that will make a difference and support children with SEMH needs.

I have worked in Early Years for 30 years, and – without a doubt – the work I do now is the most rewarding I have experienced. I hope I have shared with you a glimmer of the delight and wonder that I see each day with the children I work with. Yes, there are some days and weeks which can feel draining and exhausting, but mostly this is the most amazing job I have had in my career. I feel hugely privileged to be able to work with, and maybe make a small difference in, children's lives. My job is only possible because the teaching assistants, teachers, SENCOs and headteachers trust me and will try out the ideas and suggestions I offer to them. I only pop in and out of a school each week – it is the school staff who embed the ideas and make the huge difference in a child's school life in. If they were not implementing the ideas, we just wouldn't see change.

Finally, I am only able to perform my role because I am part of an incredible team – a team who are so highly experienced and knowledgeable, a team with whom I have laughed so much but also sometimes just sat and cried, and a team from whom I have learned such a great deal. This is a team who are incredibly nurturing and caring to one another, and it is only possible to do this work if one is part of such a group of people.

My parting message is this. We can all make a huge difference, and when we see the difference we make in children's lives it really is *the* most rewarding job.

Index